# STATIONS
# OF THE SPIRIT

## VICTOR CARPENTER

**Introduction by James Luther Adams**

SUNFLOWER INK
Palo Colorado Canyon   Carmel, Calif. 93923

## ACKNOWLEDGEMENTS

Permission to publish material from the following sources is hereby gratefully acknowledged.

Penguin Books Ltd., for a selection from *The Heart of the Hunter,* by Laurens van der Post; copyright 1961, by Penguin Books.

P. G. Putnam's Sons, for a section from *Lord of the Flies,* by William Golding; copyright 1954, by P. G. Putnam's Sons.

Purnell and Sons, for the poem "Idiot Child," by Sydney Clouts; copyright 1966, Sydney Clouts.

W. W. Norton Co., Inc., for lines from "Diving Into the Wreck," by Adrienne Rich; *Poems, Selected and New, 1950-1974,* copyright 1974, by W. W. Norton Co.

North Point Press, for lines from "The Peace of Wild Things," by Wendell Berry; *Openings,* North Point Press.

Library of Congress Catalogue No. 89-052162
ISBN 0-931104-28-9

# STATIONS OF THE SPIRIT

Cover Painting
by
Nathaniel Larrabee

# DEDICATION

This book is dedicated to

## Cathe

Wife, friend, lover, confidant, editor

and life companion

*"wing to wing and oar to oar"*

# TABLE OF CONTENTS

                                                              Page

Acknowledgements ............................. iv
Introduction by James Luther Adams.............. ix
Preface by Victor H. Carpenter ................... xi

*STATIONS OF THE SPIRIT:*

  **1** In The Moment ................................1
       On Being Religious ...........................3
       Paying Attention .............................6
       The Consecration of Experience ...............14
  **2** In The Liberal Ministry ........................21
       Memory and Hope ...........................23
       The Prophetic Ministry........................27
       Urban Ministry: Wilderness and Wonderland......31
  **3** In The City ...................................49
       Whose City Is It Anyway? .....................51
       So Where's The "Common Ground"?............58
       The Assassination of a City's Soul ..............64
       Afraids .....................................70
  **4** In The Company Of Persons With Disabilities .....77
       Lessons From our Daughter Gracia .............81
       "Couldn't God have Made You Better?"..........92
       Gracia II ................................... 100
  **5** In The Struggle For Racial Justice ..............107
       The Long Confusion About Black Empowerment..109
       A King and A Duke: When Images Conflict ......117
       Fascism, Racism and The Klan ................123
       The Courage of Our Contradictions ...........130
  **6** In The South African Crucible..................149
       Living In Unreality...........................151
       South Africa: Naught For Your Comfort ........159
  **7** In The Self ..................................167
       Trusting The Process ........................169
       Safety and Vulnerability: Delicate Balance .......175
       To Hear The Music When Our Own Songs Cease..180

# INTRODUCTION
James Luther Adams

G. K. Chesterton tells us that he once toyed with the notion of preparing a novel to be entitled, *The Discovery of England.* In this novel an expeditionary naval force would set out on the high seas in search of new territory to claim for St. George and the King. After a long period they with delight would sight land in the distance. After steering with expectation toward the foreign strand they would cast anchor and disembark to claim the territory, all the while thinking that the barbarous structures were of alien country and culture. But presently they would become aware of having landed at Brighton Beach on the south of England. They had "discovered" England—no small achievement, says Chesterton.

The present volume by Victor Carpenter is an expedition leading to the recognition of American society and religion in a Unitarian Universalist modality, or from that perspective, an expedition in company with Mrs. Carpenter, Cathe, the poet. Victor speaks of his denomination as "essentially white, essentially middle-economic, essentially suburban."

Throughout the book he deals with what is called "spirituality," a weasel term if ever there was one. He notes the brummagem forms of spirituality, eventually giving what is really an Augustinian definition when he asserts that spirituality refers to what we pay attention to—understood within a life structure. For Augustine, what one loves determines what one pays attention to. In this view (which is Victor's), authentic spirituality requires more than pure spirit; it becomes full-bodied, incarnate in a social, historical context. False spirituality is the spirituality of pure spirit. One is reminded here of Wordsworth's word: "I use SPIRIT to stand for total experience . . . a spirit that impels all thinking things, all objects of all thought, and rolls through all things."

The entire book, of course, reveals what the author characteristically pays attention to and calls our attention to. He speaks of the itinerary as "Stations of the Spirit." At first blush I thought of the "Stations" noted by Dante in *The Divine Comedy*, "Stations" leading not to tragedy but to happy, that is to "comic," ending. In the Roman Catholic tradition the "Stations of the Cross" articulate a progression from Christ's being condemned to death on until his body is laid in the tomb. For Victor Carpenter, however, the "Stations of the Spirit" represent moments and experiences of life-giving energy and challenge. The "Stations" alluded to are those times and places when and where his personal, spiritual journey has been awakened, nourished and re-directed—in some ways changed and enriched. These "Stations," then, are in anticipation noted in the chapter headings, from "In The Moment" on to "In The Self." The reader will be struck by the thread of conflict or struggle for racial justice, to the South African Crucible, and so on to the struggle in the Self. Yet, at each "Station" an element of victory is present. So in the Dantean sense, each "Station" and also the entire itinerary ends in "comedy."

In all of this, the author presents himself as a non-Reagan conservative, as one committed to conserving "human rights or the environment or the duties or the services to the needy." A striking thing about this journey is twofold: it is in one respect an account of happenings in the social world, and in another it is an autobiography in full detail. Thus, the objective and the subjective worlds are brought into provisional concord. And through it all we see not only tragedy, but also we hear the trumpet of the morn. Such is the vision of Victor Carpenter, set forth in lively, imaginative, pungent style—all presenting a discovery, a portrait, of America, warts and all.

James Luther Adams
Professor Emeritus
Harvard Divinity School
Harvard University
Cambridge, MA

# A PREFACE

The selections that constitute this book relate to issues that have stirred my imagination, demanded my response and shaped my perspective on our times and our purposes. Throughout my thirty-one years as a Unitarian and then as a Unitarian Universalist minister, these issues have repeatedly confronted and challenged me with the need to learn, to change, and to act. These are not points of arrival. They are stopping places on a life journey. The "Stations" will continue to require response from me and, I suggest, from all of us, during the closing years of the 20th Century. My hope is that the experiences and such insights as I have gained from them will encourage others in preparing for our several destinations.

Several of the essays and addresses have been published elsewhere. "Urban Ministry: Wilderness and Wonderland" was originally delivered at the Unitarian Universalist General Assembly in Boston, 1978, as the James Luther Adams Lecture. It was subsequently published in *The Right Time: The Best of Kairos,* David Parke, ed., Skinner House, 1982. "The Courage of Our Contradictions" was published in 1983 as the last of four lectures sponsored by the Minns Foundation under the collective title, *The Black Empowerment Controversy and the Unitarian Universalist Association.* "Living in Unreality" was published in *The Boston Phoenix,* July 12, 1985.

I want to express my thanks to the members of those congregations which I have been privileged to serve who have nurtured, stimulated, forgiven and empowered me in our years together: the members of Christ Church, Dorchester, MA, where I was ordained in 1958; the First Parish in Norwell, MA; The Free Protestant Church of South Africa, Cape Town, S.A.; The First Unitarian Church of

Philadelphia, PA; the Arlington Street Church, Boston, MA; and presently, the First Unitarian Church of San Francisco, San Francisco, CA.

To the wonderfully skillful Melinda Lee, who typed the manuscript and saw it through its several drafts with astonishing good cheer, my gratitude unbounded.

To Cathe Carpenter who edited the manuscript, advised and shaped its contents, and provided material for the disabilities section, my heartfelt thanks.

Victor H. Carpenter
November, 1989

# STATIONS OF THE SPIRIT

REFLECTIONS, ESSAYS AND ADDRESSES

# 1

# ...IN THE MOMENT

# ON BEING RELIGIOUS

Religious faith is expressed on many levels. These levels are not of equal nor even of evident worth. It is therefore essential to make distinctions. My preferred means for making distinctions is by holding up the various expressions of faith to the *larger light* supplied by the experience of individuals who have made religion authentic for me.

Rather than asking, "What is religious faith," I ask, "What is it about a certain person — Malcolm X, or Dorothy Day, Nelson Mandela, or Sophia Lyon Fahs that moves me to think of him or her as being religious?" What is intimated by their lives that is of worthy consequence for the way I live and for the hopes I have for the lives of my family, my community, my world.

One common element emerges: the religious life of each has been characterized by their vivid sense of *vocation*. This vivid sense of vocation is capsuled in such classic stories as that of Jesus' baptism, of Moses confronted by the burning bush, of Gautama under the Bo tree. It was at his baptism that Jesus experienced the assurance that in the vast scheme of things he was being depended upon to carry through a most important work, a vocation, a mission. It should be noted that in none of the cases cited was the nature of the important work clear.

The awareness of vocation does not guarantee either the wisdom or the success of the way in which the response is made. But that wisdom or success does not truly matter. Jesus was religious *not* because he was particularly successful. He was religious because he made a generous and heroic response to the experience of vocation. Exactly the same thing can be said for Malcolm X, Dorothy Day, Sophia Fahs, Nelson Mandela, Mohandas Ghandi, Albert

3

Schweitzer, Mother Theresa, Mohammed, Guatama Buddha, and so many others.

Religious faith begins in our recognition of — and our respect for — this experience of vocation when we see it manifested. Religious faith quickens as that experience of vocation comes to each of us. When we are addressed . . . called. . . summoned, by words or experience similar to the expression which came to Jesus: "*Thou* art my beloved child. . . so live, that in thee *too* I shall be well pleased."

The experience of vocation is the beginning of a religious life, not the end. Growth in the religious living cannot be guaranteed. It requires nurture and support in a compatible environment. Going to a particular church does not automatically signify that we receive an adequate expression of vocational community. The right kind of church is one in which members are continually being reminded of the larger call upon them — and continually being assisted in responding to that larger call in terms of opportunity and action. The right kind of church is one in which members will be afforded opportunities to grow in their expression of religious vocation. The right kind of church fosters and encourages the creative play of the imagination, calling members to accept new challenges, wherever those challenges present themselves. As Unitarian Universalists, we have the advantage of bearing traditions which have always appreciated the central place of community in religion. Unitarian Universalists are religious liberals who believe in the church as a vehicle for the expression of vocation.

The distinguished English Unitarian L. P. Jacks once said that life is best studied in the form of dialogue.

"Will you live?" The question comes to us, and as infants, not understanding what we are doing, we eagerly answer, "Yes, we will live." Later, when we have become aware of what is involved, we are again asked, "Will you live?" And again, with all of our tenacity and perseverance, we reply,

4

"Yes, we will live." But then life asks another question: "How will you live? What kind of person will you be?" We do not answer these two questions verbally. We answer by what we choose and by what we reject, we answer by what we love and by what we destroy. To hear these questions, and to respond to them with generous, loving and brave answers — that is what "being religious" means.

# PAYING ATTENTION

Laurens Van Der Post's book, *The Heart of the Hunter,*
contains a tale that combines a myth and a dream of southern Africa. There is a beauty and a wisdom about the tale,
and it deserves attention. What follows is a simplified
version:

> *There was a man of the early race who dearly loved
> his cattle. He always took them into the veldt and
> chose the best possible grazing for them and watched
> over them, seeing that no wild animal could come
> near to hurt or disturb. And in the evening he would
> bring them back to his kraal, seal the entrance care-
> fully with branches of the toughest thorn, and watch
> them contentedly chewing their cud thinking: "In the
> morning I shall have wonderful rich milk to drink."*
>
> *One morning, however, when he went to his kraal,
> expecting that the udders of the cows would be full
> and sleek with milk, he was amazed to find them slack
> and empty and dry, and he thought, with immediate
> self-reproach, that he had chosen their grazing badly
> and he took them to better grass and he brought them
> home that evening again thinking: tomorrow I shall
> certainly have good milk. But again, on the following
> morning the cows' udders were slack and dry. And for
> the second time he changed their grazing and yet the
> cows still gave no milk.*
>
> *Disturbed and suspicious, he decided to keep
> watch upon his cattle that night, and in the middle of
> the night he was astonished to see a cord of finely
> woven fiber descending from the stars, and down the
> cord, hand over hand came, one after another, young
> women of the people of the sky.*
>
> *He saw them, beautiful and lithe, whispering and*

6

*laughing among themselves, he saw them steal into his kraal and milk his cattle dry. Indignant, he jumped out to catch them but they scattered cleverly so that he did not know which way to run. But in the end he did manage to catch one, but while he was chasing her the rest fled up the sky and withdrew the cord after them so that he could not follow.*

*However, he was content because the young woman he had caught was the loveliest of them all and he made her his wife and from that moment, he had no more trouble from the people in the sky. His new wife went happily to her daily tasks and they were happy together and they prospered. There was only one thing that worried him. When he caught his wife she had a basket with her. It was skillfully woven, so tight that he could not see through it and it was always closed firmly on top with a lid that fitted exactly over the opening. Before she would marry him his wife had made him promise that he would never lift the lid of the basket and look inside until she gave him permission to do so. If he did, she warned, a great disaster might overtake them.*

*But as the months went by the man began to forget his promise, he became steadily more curious about the basket, seeing it near day by day and always with the lid firmly shut, and then one day, when he was alone, and his wife was out, he saw the basket standing there in the shadows and he could bear it no longer. Snatching off the lid he looked inside. For a moment he stood there unbelieving and then he burst out laughing.*

*And when his wife came, in the evening, she knew what had happened and she put her hand to her heart and looked at him with tears in her eyes, and said, "You have looked in the basket." And he admitted it with a laugh and he said: "Why you silly, silly creature! Why have you made such a fuss about the basket, there's nothing in it."*

*"Nothing," she said, hardly finding the strength to speak. "Yes, nothing," he answered emphatically. At that she turned her back on him, walked away straight into the sunset and vanished and was never seen again.*

Why did she leave? Because he had broken his promise about looking in the basket? I doubt it. I believe she left because when he looked in the basket he found it empty.

The basket was not empty. The basket was filled with beautiful things that she had stored from her people in the sky, to be shared with him when he had the eyes to see them and the ability to wonder over them. Because he had not seen them and had just laughed at what he perceived to be the emptiness of the basket she saw that there was no place for her or for her gifts.

The story is a moving expression of what I call a crisis in spirituality in the industrialized world today. The crisis results from not knowing what things are of worth or where to look or when to pay attention. Each of us is the farmer in the story. We sneak a peek into the basket called "spiritual- ity." Too often we see what our consumerist culture condi- tions us to see.

"Forty ways to increase our spiritual power." "Pray your- self thin." "Mantras for the middle class." "I was a guru for the FBI." "How God helped me make millions in real estate."

Our society pushes images at each of us. Images to enhance our personal economic growth. We all know them (e.g., Get ahead; do your own thing; be all that you can be). These images are highly individualistic, highly competitive and absolve one of concern for a wider social justice. These have become the habits of our hearts.

Bad habits! But bad from the standpoint that they will never permit us to see anything except emptiness in that mythic basket in our midst. Bad habits growing up around the idea of spirituality can be replaced by good habits. A good place to start replacing them is to return to the idea of spirituality itself.

The word "spirituality" originally appeared in English in the 17th Century but it is much older than that. The root of the word "spirit" goes back to many languages in addition to Hebrew. Akin to the Latin, "spirare" (to breathe), it means "breath." Spirit is equated with the breath of life. The inspirited body, the living human being, is a concept which belongs to the genesis in human consciousness of the fact of human existence.

The separation of spirit from the organic body was a much later development. This separation resulted in all of these dualistic splits that we are all familiar with: nature vs. history, mind vs. body, spirit vs. matter, and dozens more. What has been lost in that dualism is the image of the spirit of God moving over the face of the earth as it was captured in the book of Genesis. That image echoes the earliest strata of human consciousness of how creation occurs when into the undifferentiated is breathed the breath, the spirit of life, and life in all of its riotous profusion breaks out.

I love that image. I love it because it weds the spirit to the totality of life. I love it because it helps me to remember that spirituality is not something separated from the world but something that deeply affects the way we live and move and have our being *in the world*.

People often fail in their attempts to experience spiritual renewal. I suspect they forget to incorporate the spiritual renewal into their life "structure." Life structure, a phrase coined by the psychiatrist Daniel Levinson, first appeared in his book, *The Seasons of a Man's Life*. Levinson expresses the point that "life structure" is bound up with what we pay attention to. One could do a significant analysis of a person's life simply by rifling through his/her checkbook: books bought during the past year; tickets to events attended; charitable contributions made...

Out of an intuitive grasp of life's structure a student in Ireland commented that he could analyze the social situation of the church leadership in his country if he knew where

9

Ireland's bishops ate when they took their meals away from home, with whom they ate, and who picked up the tab. The context of his concern was that he believed Irish bishops to be totally out of touch with the unemployed young people of his country. He was probably right.

Our spirits are shaped by what we pay attention to even when currents flow in a different direction than we might anticipate or prepare for.

A story of spiritual awareness and spiritual responsiveness in unexpected circumstances appeared in the Op-Ed page of the *New York Times* during the time of the 1988 Presidential primary campaigns. The author told of being with his brother in a waiting room of a Los Angeles hospital where the brother's wife was fighting for her life in an adjacent room. The two men heard a commotion and looked to see candidate Jesse Jackson and his entourage sweeping into the hospital corridor. Jackson and company stuck their heads in the waiting room; the author assured Jackson they were both card-carrying Democrats, and Jackson quipped, "Get their cards," then continued on his way to pay a brief visit to Bill Cosby's mother, who was recuperating in that hospital.

The author's brother wondered if Jackson might be prevailed upon to step into his wife's hospital room and say a prayer for her recovery. They met the Jackson entourage as they were returning down the corridor on to the next appointment. They made the request. Jackson's handlers said: "No, the plane won't wait! You just can't do it, Jesse." But Jackson, without hesitation, brushed aside his handlers, went into the designated hospital room where the woman lay in a semi-coma, took the woman's hand, and started to pray.

Sensitive to the fact that the woman, her husband, and the author of the article were all Jews, he couched his prayer with references to Judaism and not Christianity. The author quoted the beginning of the prayer as saying: "God, you brought the children of Israel out of the land of Egypt, you protected Daniel in the lion's den, God, we need another

10

miracle here." He prayed for about two minutes, holding the woman's hand. When he finished, he went over to the brother, who by this time was dissolved in tears. Jackson put his arm around him, embraced him, held him for the period that it took him to regain his composure, and was gone.

I suggest that Jesse Jackson's pre-emption of the campaign schedule to perform a personal task of ministry was neither a publicity stunt nor out of character. His sensitive prayer for the stricken woman and his stump speech for justice are all of a piece. Both come from a life structure in which spirituality has a critical, socially integrative place.

A privatized, separated, interiorized spirituality cannot bring about righteousness or do the work of justice in the world. It cannot help to integrate the deep passion for love and justice in our spiritual lives.

Theologian Karl Rahner wrote, "Spirituality is a mysterious and tender thing about which we can speak only with the greatest difficulty." Rahner's statement is good counsel, particularly for people like me for whom things spiritual are a professional stock in trade. We "spiritual professionals" tend to be glib and less likely to reflect upon the kind and quality of spirituality asked of us.

If spiritualty is indeed a matter of knowing what to pay attention to, what is it that I pay attention to? My home is located on top of one of San Francisco's wonderful hills. On Mt. Olympus, in fact! It has a panoramic view across the city and Golden Gate Park, all the way to the Pacific. Not long ago, in my living room, a group of ministers gathered (as we do on a regular basis) to touch, support and, if need be, to heal each other's wounds. We check in and share the stuff of our lives.

On this occasion one clergyperson spoke about a particularly difficult period in her life, marked by profound stress and conflict. As she was describing her struggle to deal with the pressures and conflicts of her life, I was seized by the sight of a very large, black crow framed by my window behind her. It was making huge sweeping arcs, back and forth, across the expanse. While frequently visited by birds, I had no memory of seeing a crow there before, and such a large crow, tracing and retracing its path. It seemed to demand that I pay attention - but to what?

I resolved the conflict by breaking in upon the minister's recitation to tell of the crow. At a level of awareness I confess not to understand, it felt like a hopeful sign, a sign of balance for her.

After our meeting ended, the conjunction of the woman's anguish and the crow's flight stayed with me, as if urging that I continue to pay attention, to pay closer attention, to see more than what met my eye. So I began to reflect on that crow and on crows in general.

Crows usually get "a bad press." They do not sing and they are not particularly attractive. One thinks of crows' first cousin, Edgar Allen Poe's raven; one thinks of crows usually as ominous, harbingers of ill-fate. But crows are not always ominous, and this particular crow was not ominous. In its sweeping, soaring presence it conveyed something to me of liberation, of freedom, of joy. As I spoke of its presence the expression on my colleague's face changed from anguish to a look resembling appreciation and acceptance.

Days later, I remembered how Rev. Harry Scholefield, Minister Emeritus of the First Unitarian Society of San Francisco, had told me of his own special fondness for crows; how they are companionable creatures; how they represent a fundamental survival tenacity in living things. The crow's tenacity can represent the ability to rise above that which is crippling and demeaning, stultifying and life-strangling.

And thus I am moved to praise the consciousness of creation that succeeded in breaking through my matter-of-fact-dailiness to gift me with a crow's flight and a woman's plaint, prompting awareness that the one could make a deep, significant difference to the other and to me. Spirit, spirituality; it is a matter of paying attention to what the basket contains.

> *"And higher far and far more clear*
> *Thee in our spirit we behold*

> *Thine image and thy self are there*
> *Indwelling God proclaimed of old."*

# THE CONSECRATION OF EXPERIENCE

If someone asked me to name one truly spiritual book, written in the 1980's decade, I would answer without hesitation, *The Color Purple*, by Alice Walker. I would cite the passage in which the jazz singer, Shug, in wonderfully salty language, awakens Celie's wonder and astonishment at the spiritual significance that is waiting to be found in the natural world and in the things of her own personal experience. That same insight moved e. e. cummings to proclaim: "i thank you God for this most amazing day." It moved Gerard Manly Hopkins to write that the world is charged with the glory of God, it will "flame out like shining from shook foil." But for all the wisdom which we can elicit from poets and novelists about the spiritual significance of the natural world, the discovery is still something we each must make on our own, within the context of our unique experience.

For me the instrument of discovery was chestnuts—horse chestnuts. If you come from the Mid-west you probably call them buckeyes, but if you are from New England they are horse chestnuts. I have a vivid memory of a large horse chestnut tree that grew close to my grandmother's house when I was growing up, and how in the fall, when the chestnuts fell to the ground, I would collect them. Those who know about horse chestnuts know that the nut itself is wrapped in a spiny shell. With considerable skill and dexterity you break open the shell in order to extract the chestnut. Inside the shell is a kind of white, silky substance which acts as a bed for the chestnut. As you extract the rich auburn-brown and smooth nut from its bed you discover that the texture is almost liquid.

As a child I can remember collecting these wonderful objects. A couple of hours of picking and careful shelling would produce a shoe-box full. I would contemplate all the wonderful things that I could do with them.

But sooner or later reality interrupted the fantasy. Those familiar with these natural beauties know that you can do nothing with them. You cannot eat, cook or even peel them. Every time you cut through that splendid, sensual skin you encounter a kind of a pulpy muck. All you can do with horse chestnuts is throw them away.

And yet the following year I would go out and again gather horse chestnuts! You could say I was a slow learner, and I must admit that I did not fully appreciate or understand the power which these things had over me. It was only years later that I came to realize that these horse chestnuts were really doors of perception, awakening me to the fact that there is more to the natural world than meets the eye or is grasped in the hand. To discover that the earth has treasures with an unfathomable power to awaken profound wonder in us is to discover the spirit at work in the world.

Things of the earth are entrances into the realm of the spirit. We touch them, stumble over them or fall into them as Alice tumbled down that rabbit hole. We slide into the labyrinthine resonances. The spiritual is not a discrete category within human experience. The spiritual is a quality that has the power to pervade and amplify *all* human experience. The spiritual is the consecration of experience so that the full significance of that experience resonates in our imagination.

One aspect of *The Color Purple* that defines it as a spiritual book is its very earthiness. The saltiness in the telling. Spirituality, divorced from the commonplace of life, ought to be viewed with suspicion. It is unfortunate that spirituality is so often associated with the sentimental and superficial. The sentimental and the superficial tend to lull, desensitize, and stupefy us. Spirituality should have precisely the opposite effect. It should awaken, excite, arouse us. It should stir us out of our inclination to be complacent. Spirituality is to complacency what life is to death.

I carry in my memory the vision of two national memorials, both of which are spiritual in intent, but only one of which conveys true spiritual power. The first memorial sits

15

on top of a small hill located about five miles south of the city of Pretoria in South Africa. It is a massive, ponderous concrete fortress. This fortress commands the landscape for miles in all directions. This monolith, enclosed by a concrete base relief of wagons inside a wrought iron fence of spears, is approached by a long staircase. The stairs lead to a door at the base of the monument. The visitor climbs the staircase, enters and discovers a cavernous space, empty except for a large block of marble placed in the center of the floor. There are no windows. Nothing to allow the light of day to enter, save for one small opening located in the monument's roof. This memorial has been engineered to accord with the earth's movement so that on a particular day of the year, the 16th of December, the sun will be positioned to shine a ray of light through that aperture. The light will fall precisely on the center of the block of marble.

The site is called the Voortrekker Monument. It was built to celebrate the spirit of Afrikanerdom. It symbolizes the military victory of the Afrikaner settlers over the Zulu tribe, which occurred on the 16th of December, 1838. The monument's purpose is to remind the individual Afrikaner of Afrikanerdom's unbending, unyielding commitment to doctrines of racial superiority and to their vision of themselves as "chosen people." Each year, in the monument's shadow, Afrikaners gather to celebrate the determination and rigid self-control that has sustained them in the past and which they believe will carry them into the future.

The other national memorial of spiritual purpose does not rise from a hill. It is cut into a valley. The Vietnam Memorial in Washington, D.C. is a deep, dark valley of remembrance about a war that our nation would prefer to forget. Created by a 21-year-old woman of Asian inheritance, it is an inescapable reminder of the 59,000 Americans and the hundreds of thousands of Asians who were that war's victims.

Both the Voortrekker Monument outside of Pretoria and the Vietnam Memorial in Washington, D.C. are spiritual in their motivation and intent. The difference is in the conception of spirituality that each proclaims. The Voortrekker

Monument speaks to a nationalistic piety, a "God-on-our-side" mind set. It is geared to submerge the individuality of the visitor in the tribal identity of a "volk," precluding opportunity for self-questioning or self-assessment of personal responsibility. By contrast, the Vietnam Memorial demands personal ackowledgement and response. In its presence you cannot be complacent. The wall says, 'Here is your humanity," and our tears, anger, bitter grief, deep sorrow ackowledge that truth. Such acknowledgment is the hallmark of spiritual authenticity. Anything that awakens you to an awareness of the depth and significance of your own experience is spiritual.

Our culture is not geared to produce spiritual encounters. Our culture is geared to put us to sleep. It proclaims, "There is no God but torpor, and television is its prophet." Fred Allen spoke truth when he referred to TV as "chewing gum for the eyes." Social critic Neil Postman has written about the soporific effects of television. His study, *Amusing Ourselves To Death*, is not an attack on television per se. In fact, the author is highly complimentary about much of what television produces in the areas of advertising and entertainment. The ads, he says, are particularly creative in an imaginative, glitzy kind of way. The ads are the most interesting part of television. TV is pernicious when it takes itself seriously.

A case in point: the American Broadcasting Company's production several seasons ago of a program called *The Day After*. It was a mini-series which purported to address disasters occurring in a particular American community in the wake of a nuclear attack. The production was preceded by much ballyhoo and flackery. This was *serious* television. Churches received study kits. People were encouraged to watch the series in groups because isolation might produce anxiety and psychic trauma. Hospitals were urged to alert psychiatric staffs and be prepared to deal with the shock that was going to occur after people watched *The Day After*. The political right huffed and puffed, charging the American Broadcasting Company with a communist inspired plot to subvert this country's fighting resolve by showing how Americans would be totally demoralized by a nuclear attack. Serious hype!

The production turned out to be nothing but standard television melodrama. Utterly forgettable. The series not only lacked power to awaken anyone to the horrors of nuclear war; it had precisely the opposite effect. It made the viewing audiences all the more complacent about the greatest danger facing the human community at this point in our history.

*The Day After* is another instance of psychic numbing that grips us when we seriously contemplate nuclear war. Complacency, psychic numbing, social amnesia; these are the forces which deaden, demean, and destroy our personal experience. These are the forces which are enemies of anything one could remotely call spiritual. The Dutch Jesuit theologian Henri Nouwen commented, "Our great task is not to let the power of death manipulate us. Our great task is to live in this death-oriented world without letting death pollute us."*

Toward the end of his tragically short life, John Lennon wrote a song called *Imagine* in which he encouraged us to exercise our powers of imagination and wonder, that we might envision what it would be like to live in a peaceful, war free world. He encouraged us to be *imaginal*. It is an encouragement that needs repeating because "imaginal" is so easily confused with words that sound like "imaginary" and "imaginative." The three words have distinct and separate meanings. For example, *The Wind in the Willows*, is an "imaginative" story, populated with "imaginary" beings (Ratty, Mole, Mr. Toad)! But those are not the reasons for its hold upon us. The fact that *The Wind in the Willows* continues to live in literature depends not on the story or the characters but upon the "imaginal" world into which our reading allows us to enter and in which we are permitted full participation.

Is the imaginal world real? Re-read *The Wind In The Willows*. Join Shug and Celie as they discover the color purple in the field. Break open the shell of a horse chestnut and touch that liquid reality. Feel the quality of life stirring in the very depths of your own personal experience.

The imaginal and the spiritual are one. They consecrate our experience, complete it, codify it, give additional meaning to it. They make our lives whole and, thereby, make them holy.

*Public lecture, Boston, MA, 1986.

# 2

## ...IN THE LIBERAL MINISTRY

# MEMORY AND HOPE

(At the Ordination of The Rev. Jean Rickard
Cambridge, MA 1981)

From 1976 to 1987 I served as minister to a congregation
which has a reputation for taking social issues seriously: The
Arlington Street Church, Boston, Massachusetts. I expect
that is the reason I was invited to lead a recent denominational workshop on the topic, "Social Responsibility in a
Conservative Time." I was not happy about the workshop
title because I did not think we were living in a conservative
time. I saw the Reagan administration's claim to be conservative as deceitful. I saw no evidence of administrative effort
to conserve our human rights or the environment, to conserve the cities or services to the needy. In short, I saw no
effort to conserve anything I was interested in conserving.

This is not a conservative time. It is a forgetful time.
"Forget" is the word I have heard coming out of Washington, D.C., throughout the 1980s. If you're poor, forget housing. If you're black, forget equality. If you're a woman, forget
abortion. If you're old, forget social security. If you're
unlucky enough to live in states that want evolution taught,
you can even forget where you came from. As a people we
seem to be in a period of profound forgetfulness, marked by
failure to recall or make sense of the struggles of the past.
Derek Jacoby coined the phrase "social amnesia." I think it
describes our condition accurately.

Our social memory is anesthetized by incessant demands
of the trivial and the daily. We no longer are encouraged to
remember the noble and the transcendent. One reason
churches are so important to us now is that one of their
functions is to store memory. We go to church in order to
*remember* who and what we are. Willard Sperry, former
Dean of the Harvard Divinity School, defined the church as

"the community of memory and hope." What better time to recall this definition than when memory is in such short supply and hope seems so forlorn.

A church is a place to remember, a community of memory. A church is a place to remember communally, to co-remember, to co-memorate. The simple act of pronouncing such words as "co-memorate" provokes the memory and calls us to recognize that our society encourages us not only to "forget," but to forget in *isolation* from each other. Forgetfulness and isolation are two sides of the same coin, one reinforces the other. As we remember *together* we recognize that our society not only works *against* remembering, it encourages isolation. As we remember *together* we subvert attempts by the powers controlling our society to break us up into easily controllable monads.

The women's movement has an adage: When two women get together and discover that they have the same problems, that's a political act. It is also a religious act. Remembering together is one of the strands in our American history, bequeathed by the congregational structure of the New England churches and re-enacted in town meetings and union halls within a society that steadily presses against such forms of unity. It takes work to remember together. It takes work to create and nurture these crazy, demanding, archaic pockets of collaboration and mutual aid called churches. It is important work, particularly in a society that relies on competition and meritocracy and encourages us to stay free of commitment and promises; to keep aloof from one another; and to win, win, win, by looking after Number One.

I do not want to say or even to imply that it is wrong to go off alone to think, to meditate, to engage the silence behind the speaking. I do not think that we are in any danger of forgetting the individualistic side of any healthy community. What we need to *remember* are the ways and forms of being together *on every scale*: making decisions, having fun, consoling and rejoicing, raising children, caring for the elderly, washing the dishes, overthrowing the government.

So many of the old customs that dictated how we do these things are slipping out of memory. Like the tramps in Samuel Beckett's *Waiting for Godot* we look about us and declare, "Nothing to be done!" That is internalized oppression! Virtually *every* social analyst since Marx and Freud has observed that all oppression stems from a forgetting—individual or communal. A forgotten past does not liberate us; it holds us back. A forgotten past is a past where nostalgia has replaced memory.

William Sloane Coffin scores this kind of impotent nostalgia with an anecdote from his chaplaincy days at Yale. Addressing students about to graduate, he gruffly warned: "Watch out! Lest fifty years from now you look back on this springtime of your lives and say, "Those, those were the days!' - And be *right!*"

The church, the community of memory, the place of co-memorating, is also the place of *hoping*. Only a community that remembers can be a community that hopes. In such a forgetful time is there any wonder that there is so little hope? In a public opinion poll conducted in California in 1984, a random sampling of people were asked two questions: Do you believe that there will be a nuclear war? Do you believe that you will survive it? To the astonishment of the polltakers, 84% of the respondents said "yes," they believed there would be nuclear war, and "no," they didn't believe that they would personally survive. I can think of no more devastating testimony to endemic hopelessness. And you cannot dismiss those results as just reflecting California. Theologian Harvey Cox reports that he took his own poll asking students in a variety of his classes at Harvard University the same questions and got essentially the same results.

If the same two questions were addressed to you, how would you answer? And how would you square your answers with your involvement and membership in a church? If you number yourself as among that 16% who believed there would *not* be a nuclear war, ask yourself how your hope is acted out in the context of your "community of memory and hope."

Communities of hope are, by definition, communities of action. Churches are among the few places we have where hope can be acted out. They are places where the social taboos against expressions of outrage can be removed and where people are encouraged to confront, to demand of, to rage against the forces of oppression and destruction—the forces of forgetfulness—that would numb and cripple and destroy. Communities that can hope are communities that can raise hell.

When thinking of a community of memory and hope it is profoundly appropriate to invoke the name of The Rev. Stephen Fritchman whose ministerial life was one long testimonial to the truth that when memory and hope are wedded in the person of an individual minister, no less than in a specific congregation, a kindling brilliance of epic proportions results. Were he alive today, Stephen would remind us of our magnificent historical task: interpreting, refining, expanding the moral meaning of religion. At the time of his death he was preparing a July Fourth address, describing the problem of teaching patriotism to the poor and the alienated of this nation.

To interpret, refine, and expand the moral meaning of religion, in a time when the values which we cherish are under vicious and well-financed attack from right wing groups who identify religion as a means of oppression, subservience, and control, is our task. What a task! What an *opportunity!*

Our theology is rooted in a faith that the affections of free, liberal religion mutually practiced makes us better people. More open, more joyful, and more loving people. While our religious community always will be a place of private deepening, it will be *more*: a temple where the values of life are upheld; a beacon for human beings learning how to live together in peace, seeking truth, demanding social justice; and finally, a community of memory and of hope, enriched with song and prayer, friends and family, works of conscience, and deeds of love.

# THE PROPHETIC MINISTRY

(At the Ordination of The Rev. John Marsh
Norwell, MA 1982)

In February 1962 I resigned from my position as minister of this church (First Parish in Norwell, MA) to take up a ministry in Cape Town, South Africa. Twenty years from now the man whom you ordain to the Unitarian Universalist ministry, The Rev. John Marsh, will be part of the Twenty-First Century. And so we move—generation unto generation.

Such circumstances stimulate the urge to forecast events; to try one's hand at predicting the future or otherwise to engage in undertakings of dubious worth. As a safeguard against falling victim to such temptation, I summon the dictum of my illustrious predecessor, The Reverend William Ellery Channing, who instructs us that the first demand of the age is neither to forecast nor to predict, but to *prophesy*. Being prophetic does not mean looking into the future but looking into the *present* with an eye prepared to discover the deep truths about that present available to the discerning eye and the inquiring mind.

The prophetic ministry to which John Marsh is ordained is a call to hold the plumb line of God's justice and God's mercy up against the society that we have constructed. The minister is called to be protaganist for the vision of a new world. The minister is called to bring searching judgment to bear upon every aspect of our local, national and international life and to call attention to those instances when and where that life runs counter to that vision of justice and mercy and hope.

But here a word of caution about the use of that judgmental plumb line. We who minister are called to *hold* it. This activity is not to be confused with *dropping* it on the heads of the congregation. When we stun parishoners with the leaden weight of our own righteous judgment we need not wonder that a congregation becomes *"soreheaded."*

A member of the First Parish of Norwell inquired about the clergy participating in John Marsh's ordination service. When informed that I had been invited to deliver the sermon, the parishoner remarked, "Oh, Carpenter! I remember him. He was a real guilt tripper!" To you, oh faithful and long suffering parishoner, I offer this heartfelt apology. As one who readily confesses to dropping his share of plumb lines I can only tell you that in the intervening years I have learned a thing or two about the use—and misuse—of that piece of surveying equipment. Principally I have learned that the demands of the age require that the plumb line of judgment be manipulated with imaginative compassion.

The call to the ministry is a call to care about the possibility of human existence and about the meanings to be discovered in the depths of that existence. The demands of the age require not only our acknowledgment, but also our entry into the dreams and the nightmares of our brothers and sisters near and far. This is compassion's agenda. Compassion is the capacity to tie our sensibilities to our neighbors' nerve endings. Compassion depends upon the imaginative caring about the joys and sorrows of those around us.

Alexander Solzhenitsyn remarked: "Mankind's sole salvation lies in everyone making everything his business." Yes, the language is sexist, and the remark is overstated, and Mr. Solzhenitsyn has some controversial ideas on other matters. *Nevertheless*, in that remark he is onto something central. Without such universal caring we are incomplete, stunted, truncated individuals. In Jesus' words, without such caring, "We are goats and not of the Kingdom."

When William Ellery Channing instructed Ezra Stiles Gannet concerning the demands of the age at that worthy's ordination in 1824, Channing placed the demand for an "enlightened ministry" in first place. I would like to believe that the demand was directed as much to the heart as to the

28

head. In my own ministry I am bombarded by facts. Facts fill my head. It spins with information about hunger, pain, sickness, runaway costs, erosion of resources. I have no trouble in getting the facts. But I have to struggle to feel what I know! I take seriously Archibald McLeish's statement, "When fact is disassociated from the feel of the fact in the minds of a people or in the common mind of a civilization, that people and that civilization is at the edge of collapse." Our age demands that we employ imaginative compassion as well as information and scholastic wisdom as we continue to live on this ever shrinking planet.

Lest anyone infer from these remarks that I place feelings above thought, the passional above the rational, let me be quick to state that this is no pitch for anti-intellectual license. It is a call to wed knowledge with compassion (which has always been understood as the mark of genuine wisdom). When Cornell University did a study of the Vietnam War one of the conclusions was that the major error we made was not in the areas of competency or technology, but in the area of imagination. Living in cities and towns that had never been bombed, we were afforded the luxury of little empathy. During the period that we were fighting a war in Southeast Asia, we were also sending men to the moon. We were able to get clear pictures of the moon and be moved and thrilled. We chose to live with blurred pictures of Southeast Asia and be unmoved and empathetically soporific.

In professional ministry one is called to deal with the real tragedy of life—not merely the facts of death, but what dies within us while we are alive; what happens to a people who cease to have compassion for all who share this planet with us. "Global village" has become a cliche, but the truth that lurks in such a cliche is readily apparent when a crisis, such as the 1982 Falkland Islands dispute between Argentina and Britain, confronts us. Nations, no less than individuals, are linked like the intricate intertwinings of a spider web. When there is disaster anywhere (even in so remote an area as the South Atlantic) an international shudder occurs, just as a web trembles when an object is hurled against it. If the force is not too intense the web merely vibrates for a while before returning to stasis. If it is violent, the web tears and hangs in ugly disarray. And when there is human triumph (often merely an act of doing what is the humanly obvious thing to do, like feeding the hungry or clothing the naked or caring for the sick) the web shimmers much as dew glistens on the web at dawn of day.

How we yearn, individually and collectively, for evidence of such triumph! For a way out of the wilderness. For rivers in the desert, order out of disorder, identity out of invisibility, honor and integrity in place of scandal and ethical recession, peace instead of war, full personhood transcending brokeness and inhuman categories. How we yearn for such triumph! How we yearn for such freedom! The age demands from its ministers examples of such triumphs, and the church ordains in the full expectation that such triumphs will be shown forth.

Yes, this vision is a tall order. But that is no excuse for failing to pursue it or for an unwillingness to incorporate it in one's life and work, however partial and inadequate that incorporation may appear. The age demands it of its ordained clergy and of its laity. Let risks be taken so that new forms of liberating human fellowship may be permitted to occur. May our ministry show the way of love, justice, salvation for all people. To make this time, our time, good time. A generative time of the living word.

# URBAN MINISTRY:
## WILDERNESS AND WONDERLAND

The city has always been an embodiment of hope and a source of festering guilt, a dream pursued and found vain, wanting, and destructive. The mood of despair over, and revulsion at, the city is certainly not new: but by this time we should have grown used to the curious psychology which urges us to look for a Utopia only to discover that where we expected that Utopia to stand we have created a hell. We sing "thine alabaster cities rise, undimmed by human tears," and readily acknowledge that our cities are dark constellations of tear-drenched misery.

Perhaps the original dream of the American city—with its plazas and avenues and Washingtonian circles—was too optimistic and elevated from reality. Perhaps the present disreputable state of "civitas" in this country is the product of an exaggerated Calvinist sense of sin and its punishments. Finding the city to be utterly irredeemable is the flip side of the expectation that it should be Paradise: utopias and dystopias go together. Disillusion is a vital part of the process of dreaming, and cynicism (as someone once remarked) is the sincerest form of sentimentality. There is something about cities which invites extremes of judgment.

The great ideal cities of history, from Plato's Republic to Le Corbusier's Radiant City, have been constructed in protest against the uninspiring conditions of cities as they actually were and, to a large degree, still are. The failures and imperfections of Athens, Rome, London, New York, Boston have inspired volume upon volume of formula cities arranged to insure humanity's greatest good. The profoundly moralistic view of the city and city life has not been exclusive property of philosophers and theologians; political

31

bosses, town planners, architects, and professional skeptics have all taken a turn at the idea of the city as a controllable option between heaven and hell.

There is something about the ideal city which authorizes us to deplore the real one, while the real city in which we pass our days continues to inspire us to create the ideal one. A 17th Century example will serve to illustrate this paradox: the city of the Sun—Civitas Solis—which was the imaginative creation of Thomas Campanella in 1623 when he was languishing in prison, a victim of the Spanish Inquisition. Campanella starts with architecture and shows us a city without people, save only the wispiest sketch figures that architects use to demonstrate the scale of a building. Campanella's city consists of seven concentric fortified circles (named for the planets) and four streets following the points of a compass. At the center is the temple of knowledge and metaphysics. Each of the seven city walls is painted with representations of various aspects of human knowledge: mathematics, botany, physics, engineering, and so forth, so that living in Campanella's city would be like inhabiting a symmetrical three-dimensional encyclopedia—a thinking person's Levittown where one is kept in a continuous state of uplift and learning.

The life which Campanella sketches in this atmosphere is crushingly puritanical and restrictive. Work is either agriculture or a cottage type industrial network of home looms and ornament making. It sounds like a rural kibbutz, and it sounds drearily familiar. We are reminded that rural nostalgia as response to the city with its merchants and entrepreneurs and its myriad of voluntary associations, gathered for labor and the assumption of responsibility, always has been treated by people who dislike cities as an unnatural perversion of the "proper scheme of things." They favor a city which accommodates itself to the seasonal rhythms and natural encounters of a rural village.

However, as Jane Jacobs has documented with brilliant insight, the myth of agricultural and rural primacy over the city lacks foundation in either archeology or economics.

Quite the contrary is true: cities enable, rather than result from, the spread of "the farm" and "the rural." I would add "the suburb," if a suburban concept can be said to have any basis beyond a mutually agreed upon conceit. The antagonism between city and suburb is merely the latest in a long line of antagonisms which stem from the conflict between the real city of our experience versus the ideal counterpart we conjure up mentally. While the antagonism may rest on a patently mythical base, the results of this antagonism have had far reaching and disastrous results for the city, its suburbs, and outlying areas.

As a case in point (one which contains comparable, if not identical, antagonisms and sequelae across this country), I draw attention to the one American city which has been historically associated with our particular religious vision and to which we repeatedly repair to touch the "sources of our strength—the rock from whence we are hewn." Boston proper has a population of just over a half a million (meager, as large cities go, it is ranked 16th on the list of major U.S. cities), but Metropolitan Boston" (ranked 5th on the list of U.S. cities) is comprised of more than a dozen separate "communities," each of which has kept its "autonomy" since the Puritans settled the area in the 17th Century. These "communities" have their own police force, schools, courts, and newspapers. Although this city has a "metropolitan economy" and certainly "metropolitan commuter routes," it has never fully coalesced into a metropolitan city.

From the restaurant-lounge on the 52nd floor of the Prudential Building you do not see the divisions and differences that make Boston what it is. You see miles and miles of what seems to be an infinitely extended small town—streets of brick houses with elm and maple trees filling the gaps between buildings stretching out to the Bay on the east and to infinity on the north, west, and south. From that vantage point you can see the majestic shape of the First Church in Roxbury, pristine upon its hill, as tidy as any suburban Unitarian-Universalist cathedral, white spired and serene. But the suburb which originally environed it turned into city.

33

Roxbury was the first, and perhaps the finest, of the 19th century "street car suburbs" of Boston. Roxbury was trees and grass and fine houses on tidy lots, the very essence of the suburban dream of village charm and amenity within easy proximity to metropolitan vigor. Today, the First church still crowns John Elliot Square, the oldest frame church in Boston, and a few of the trees are still there. As for the houses, some of them remain, but many have fallen into sullen disrepair; and our century has added rows of brick shacks where bailbondsmen and pawn brokers do their trade, and the dismantled wrecks of Fords and Buicks and Chevrolets are jacked up on blocks in the streets. One sees a few white faces and many black ones. Roxbury the suburb is now Roxbury the city. The question that Roxbury poses is not what or where is a suburb, but rather *when* and then *why* is a suburb?

During the 1860s and 1870s the suburbs of Roxbury and its sister, Dorchester, voted to annex themselves to the central city and thereby share in its bigness and its cosmopolitan bustle, its liveliness. But the "annexation movement" then reversed itself. Brookline voted to stay separate, as did Cambridge, Somerville, and others. Each vote to remain separate was a vote for the suburban myth of the independent village that was self-contained and self-reliant. The "village dweller" may, indeed, acknowledge need for the enlarged economy of the city; the technology of the city, the social and cultural amenities of the city, but his/her fundamental allegiance is to an area we call a "neighborhood" to which is attributed a specific character, while the city remains an abstraction—vague, impersonal, foreign, and threatening.

The result is a crazy quilt of town lines that enmeshes Boston and flies in the face of visible facts. As the city spreads to envelop and congeal, "village dwellers" rigorously cling to their neighborhood "communities" which are actually their own nostalgic dreams and historical anachronisms. But hold them they do, and with the help of local taxes; so that in 1976 the town of Brookline was able to spend $2,235 per pupil per school year while Somerville (located less than two miles away) only managed to scrape up $918, a difference of over $1,300.[1] There are similar inequities of expenditure of policing, street lighting, garbage disposal, and fire fighting services. Taxes diverted in the interest of an ideology are powerful weapons, and the boundaries which separate one "village" from its neighbor are simply and effectively enforced by a system of tax differentials.

What is the driving force responsible for the creation of such an anomalous situation? Is it the dream of an independent life at some safe remove from the destructive abstraction of the city? There is no doubt that such dreams are dreamt in Brookline and Newton and further out in Sudbury and Framingham; but they are also dreamt in South Boston and in Charlestown and on Beacon Hill. The constituent parts of Boston, secure in their individualist and independent mythologies, are so separated and inequitably served that it is almost impossible to imagine them coming together and actually affirming themselves as an integral part of a whole—a "city." Expressways and rapid transit systems will not connect them to each other in any meaningful way when the "proper Bostonian's" habit of mind is superstitiously bent on distancing from the larger heterogeneous environs and sticking with his or her "village."

And yet to describe the situation in terms of "dreams" and "village myths" may be only a comfortable way of avoiding the city's unpleasant meaning. My friends of Marxist persuasion point out that cities are not just ideas or dreams, but the result of the economic transformation of the United States into an industrial, class stratified, urban society. Cities, with their extremes of wealth and poverty, are the visible manifestations of the unequal workings of our capitalist society, and their residential patterns reflect the class and racial division which constitute the very core of American society and the human exploitation that proceeds from such division.

This is a difficult argument to ignore, particularly when it is borne out in one of the most astute and least compromising works to appear on the cities of this country in our time, Sam Bass Warner's *The Urban Wilderness*. Warner makes the acute observation that "for generations we have dwelt in a self-created urban wilderness of time and space, confounding ourselves with its lusty growth and rising to periodic alarms in the night. It is no accident that we have no urban history."[2]

The cruel truth is that we do have an unofficial urban history which we who dwell in some proximity to that "wilderness" would prefer to neglect or ignore because of its painful nature. Cathe Carpenter confronts us with such truth when she writes:

> *We avert our eyes from*
> *the shopping bag women,*
> *squatters on life's leftovers,*
> *who edge along*
> *blood brown gutters*
> *abutting sidewalk history*
> *stained*
> *with acrid rain*
> *waiting to catch*
> *the purveyors of change*
> *who live selling trips*
> *to nowhere from nowhere.*[3]

The unofficial history is apparent in the faces of those who dwell in Roxbury and in all the other exploited "Roxburys" across this country. It is present and predictive of the future in the uncollected garbage, uneducating schools, the unhealthful hospitals. Our "urban history" is a history of exploitation of white over black, of men over women, of rich over poor. In each of the contradictions between suburban social amenity and urban social disgrace the manisfestations of this history are apparent. Our cities are, without exception, historic and contemporary citadels of racism, classism and sexism; and since our cities are merely yesterday's suburbs, the future of these suburbs and suburban dwellers will be marked by the same anti-social, anti-human themes which they inherited from the past. The very existence of suburbs makes a profound statement about these urban "ills": Is the word "city" just another name for "poor?" Is the word "urban" just another name for "underclass?" The growing exploitation of cities by institutions of education and gentrified enclaves complicates and obfuscates the urban plight. They do not resolve the deep ills that continue to grow in our urban centers.

We fear our cities as we fear the darker sides of our own natures. As religions of the past and present manipulated fear in order to exercise control over the fearful "believer," so our fears of the city are manipulated and exploited in order that we not look too closely or ask too many questions. If we did, we might detect that the enormous wealth of the cities is being managed for the benefit of small but not invisible elites. The banking practice of "redlining;" the suburban housing pattern the banks are endorsing and encouraging with the help of the Federal Housing Authority (FHA); the systematic exclusion of particular sections of the city from political process; the creation of cheap land slumland, bulldozed and barren in preparation for new entrepreneurial advances—are all examples of "urban colonization" by which the wealth and resources of the city go to enrich the few at the expense of the many.

Our failure to perceive such a readily apparent truth results less from a willful refusal on our part than from the skewed vision of the city which our culture has encouraged us to accept. To borrow Robert Heilbroner's telling metaphor, we see the city only "through a systematic distortion introduced into the social universe by the prescriptions ground into our social spectacles."[4]

While we may lack urban history we have no shortage of urban mythology—mythology in the most negative sense of that word: a willful deception. Urban mythology is succinctly summarized in a single paragraph by theologian Max

Stackhouse:

*The failure of today's urban peoples to produce a more livable environment is their fault, inwardly caused by constitutional incapacity or a distorted sense of motivation, discipline, work habits or initiative. When and if urban peoples show that they deserve reward, our social system is so geared to reward the deserving. Of course, there are elderly people and the disabled in the city who are victims of circumstances beyond their control, and we have to develop charity programs to deal with them; but the radically improvident adults who are seen as the core of the city and who are seen as constantly demanding more attention, money and services, must be neglected until they shape up - neglected in a "benign" manner, of course.*[5]

Stackhouse goes on to point out that this gross and vicious lie is profound not only because it is articulated and believed in high government places, but also because it touches very deep places in our religious and social sensibility.

Speaking before the 1978 National Hearing of the Urban Bishops Coalition called in response to the urban crisis, sociologist Gibson Winter's statement was both perceptive and sobering:

*My own view is that we are not facing a crisis in the sense that we are dealing with an immediate problem which can be resolved through sufficient effort. I believe we are dealing with a degenerative disease that is approaching a critical stage. This disease can no longer be confined to urban areas. It will destroy our whole society if it continues. It has already wreaked havoc on every level of urban life ... Through most of Western history the cities were the centers of religious life. The inversion of this process should give us some warning of what is in store. We may be seeing the end of a 5,000 year period of experimentation with urbanism. This degenerative disease is touching every phase of our national life and corrupting societies all across the globe ...*[6]

There really are no words to describe the dimensions of such a tragedy as Winter envisions. Consider what the city is!

The city, as a socio-political formation, marked a profound transition in human history, from a time when the bonds of relationship were based exclusively on kinship to a time when human relationships could be far more comprehensive. Cities, as markets and centers for political and military activity, served to bring people together in ways which weakened and eventually brought an end to interpersonal relations based solely on blood or clan or tribe. Max Weber has argued that in accomplishing this feat, cities are incipiently "rationalizing." They constitute a social and political order which is based on reason rather than on magically manipulated taboos. The city is thus a liberating place in which people are freed from the belief that "blood" or "race," "education," "income level," "housing" are the only things that matter.

Whatever else the city is, it is a place where *different* people come together to seek and to discover new ways of being together. Thus, when it first emerged in the context of the ancient world, the city was a revolutionary event. It remains a revolutionary event today. That people could and can perceive that their hope, strength, and freedom lies not in their protection of their similarities but in their willingness to embrace their differences remains a profound and astonishing truth. It points beyond itself to a belief in the universalism of a God whose love incorporates the human race in *all* of its incredible variety/whose grace embraces all of humanity without exception/and whose kingdom (if we still can use that tarnished and misappropriated symbol) means neither the end nor the obliteration but the transfiguring of every *truly human* expression.

Articulating what is perhaps the fundamental truth upon which his concepts of power (the right to define reality) and freedom depend, Professor James Luther Adams has asserted that, "Humanity is essentially associational and human history is the history of associations. The history of

39

any open society is the history of the changing character of the associations and the changing relations between the individual and the associations, and the changing relations among the various associations."[7]

At a 1972 Unitarian-Unversalist Center City Church Conference in Philadelphia, The Rev. Jack Mendelsohn reaffirmed the importance of this associational principle as it underlies both our church polity and our theology. Dr. Mendelsohn pointed out that our associational theology is particularly appropriate to the urban milieu where humanity's differences, and the tensions which exist between those differences, are affirmed by the delicate web of associations in which they are held.[8]

In the intervening years that message of associationalism has been ignored or grossly distorted. The "diversity" about which we speak incessantly and which we are repeatedly enjoined to "celebrate" has degenerated into a glorification of the frivolous and the trivial—a self-congratulatory narcissism that beguiles us and prevents us from identifying the deadening conformity and sameness of those with whom we are in easy, flaccid, and undemanding togetherness.

Unitarian-Universalist General Assembly resolutions no longer break new ground. They serve only to reinforce positions which we have repeatedly taken in the past, and they provide, by their very dullness, a mirror of our current denomination—*the bland leading the bland.* We are an essentially white, essentially middle economic, essentially suburban-oriented denomination. In our adult membership of 150,000, I doubt that there are 1,000 African-American members; of our more than 900 clergypersons in fellowship, less than two dozen are black. Like the rest of white America, we too are tired and bored and angry at being reminded of the racism which continues to exert its stranglehold upon the life of our denomination and this society. We too are bored and annoyed by voices and issues not of our choosing which rise to confront us with unpleasant and disconcerting facts about other people's needs—need for work, need for health care, need for living space and playing space, need for response to mental, physical, and emotional handicaps. We who have achieved a measure of economic security and for whom such needs are commonplace facts of life would prefer to turn away rather than be goaded to contemplation and action in response to them.

The depth and extent of the anger that is abroad in the land is abundantly clear in the seismic shock waves emanating from California and rolling across the country in the form of proposition 2½ or 13 and others. What is being called a protest by taxpayers against governmental expenditure and bureaucratic waste is, in fact, a statement of rage on the part of those who appear to have (or believe themselves to have) some measure of economic security against those who have none. A CBS poll taken shortly after the passage of Proposition 13 revealed the confusion of those who voted in favor of drastic reduction in property taxes. Almost 70% of those interviewed felt that it would be beneficial to cut welfare payments and other expenditures allocated for the poor, but were unable to comprehend that the reduction in governmental spending power would produce cuts in social services that are useful to these home owners, such as police and fire protection. Proposition 13 is a pathetic example of people who live in today's suburb attempting to protect themselves from being engulfed by what they perceive to be the city. It is simply a footnote in the most recent chapter of our continuing abandonment of and distaste for our urban areas and what those areas represent to us.

I would like to believe that Unitarian Universalists in California and in the remaining 49 states have attained a level of social enlightenment sufficient to protect them from the siren songs, the false and empty promises of those sponsoring such regressive legislation as prototyped in proposition 13. I am, however, less sanguine about denominational willingness to confront, challenge, or see through our prevailing economic myth, namely that the United States is essentially a middle class society. That myth—and our unthinking acceptance of it—is largely responsible for our exploitation, abandonment of, and distaste for our urban areas.

According to the myth of the U.S. as a middle class society, cities are the locale of the under-class. Those who have achieved any degree of economic security are thereby granted the "right" (translate: power) to distance themselves from those who remain powerless, in the conviction that "distance" (geographic and/or economic) will be sufficient to keep "us" safe from "them."

Was there ever a time when American society did conform to the mythic contours of the "middle class image?" Was there a time, perhaps before the rise of our great metropolitan areas, when the labor force of this country was, in the main, self-employed and in control of their work (which I suggest as a meaningful and workable definition of "middle classness")? I doubt it. And I doubt if there was ever a time when some myth justifying the separation of the *laboring class* from the *slave class* was not in effect.

We beguile ourselves with romantic notions of an America comprised of farms and small villages and independent enterprise carried on by stalwart yeomen in the Jeffersonian mold. But such a description of this country, together with whatever dubious accuracy it ever might have possessed, disappeared well before the end of the 19th century.

As farming became more mechanized and was taken over by corporations, as small and independent businesses were forced to give way before the might of large and more efficient corporations, the opportunites for economic independence decreased at an accelerating rate. Already, by 1920, the self-employed work force in this country had dwindled to 25% of the population; fifty years later in 1970, that figure had shrunk to a mere 9%. In other words, the independent self-employed middle class has all but disappeared; it has been replaced by those who must depend for their livelihood upon selling their skills and their labor. At an accelerating rate during this century the character of employment opportunity has shifted from industry depend-

42

ent upon human labor to industry demanding capital investment in technology and mechanization. Perhaps the most profound result of this shift has been not the disappearance of the fact of the middle class, but rather the emergence of the "middle class" as myth and fantasy. As the power of workers to maintain control over their own work was surrendered to machine or corporation, and as workers felt themselves and their power being removed, so this class has become more and more enamored of the symbols of power and now embraces what my Presbyterian colleague, The Rev. Joe Williamson, has named "the sociology of elitism." The patterns of elitism are the patterns of upward mobility and success as determined by the values of the dominant culture. Since those values included the appearance of independence from others we divide ourselves from each other along the urban and suburban lines. But the urban/suburban divisions are only the part of the "iceberg that shows." Beneath this surface reside the profound antagonisms created along the lines of race, education, and ecomonics. Sketching in briefly how those divisions function gives us a better grasp of why the suburb is a fearful retreat from the city and why the city looms as a threatening presence to the suburb.

As technolgy increases and the mechanization of industry becomes more sophisticated, the need for unskilled and agricultural labor *decreases*. Job opportunities for those on the lowest rung of the economic ladder—the unskilled— dwindle or disappear; in our society all racial and ethnic groups have representatives in this army of unemployed, *but* it is advantageous to the economic groups one rung up on the employment ladder—the skilled and semi-skilled—to identify the lower group specifically along racial lines. The "sociology of elitism" contains a strong racist component. The unemployment and underemployment of the disadvantaged puts pressure on those with skills not to succumb to the threat of being cast into the unemployed "pit." It also means that those with sophisticated skills and levels of education consider themselves to be more firmly of the "elite" than their fellow workers who are seriously threatened by the increasing technocracy. When some at the bottom act out their frustration of powerlessness by ravaging neighborhoods that confine them, the power brokers become more adamant in their decision not to share power (via zoning requirements, etc.). Other members of the bottom rung, having acquired skills and desiring relocation in better "suburban" neighborhoods, but finding themselves blocked on the basis of race, vent their anger upon the occupants of those suburban neighborhoods.

The use of racism as a means of exacerbating antagonisms between people and preventing them from clearly examining *their* own situations vis-a-vis each other has its parallel in education. The prestige of persons with a college education who have achieved professional status—but lack social remuneration (e.g., teachers, nurses, etc.) serves to separate them from semi-skilled or non-skilled "blue collar" workers. Persons in this "professional" category have incomes which tend to be adequate (although often only barely). Persons in semi-skilled and unskilled positions on the economic ladder (black and white) feel uneasy and resentful about their own relative lack of education which results in their insecure job status because technology and automation mean fewer jobs for unskilled people. They strive to "move up" which, translated, means moving to the suburb where educational possibilities exist, if not for them, for their children.

The result of this "sociology of elitism," with its racist and educational supports, is an intense contest for dignity and status and a piece of the economic pie. It is a sociology of alienation among persons, individually and in groups, whom individuals perceive as sharing or about to share their condition. Where group solidarity occurs it is usually in terms of uniting in common defense against those perceived as threatening the privileges of a particular elite, and little attention is paid to the supremely important fact that these privileges are superficial or non-existent except to help buttress *the myth* of the middle class.

44

The artificial and often illusory distinction between the urban and the suburban has parallels in the illusory nature of the middle class myth of the suburban dream. However, there is no denying the reality of the pain and the struggle, which persons must endure once they become entrapped in the myth and its spurious promise of a good life away from the "terrors of the city."

The prophet Nahum looked down upon the collapse of his own hated city in a spirit of disdain which resembles a very contemporary attitude toward all that smacks of the urban: "Wasted is Ninevah; who will bemoan her?" And there is no shortage of passages from either Old or New Testament to buttress arguments that the city deserves to be "wasted." But such an attitude does not represent either the best or the highest in the Judeo-Christian tradition—or in our own Unitarian Universalist tradition. The book of Jonah provides a better orientation toward the city and its ministry than that of Nahum. And perhaps the tears of Jesus over Jerusalem are a more appropriate response to the ongoing urban crisis than the chorus of righteous glee over the downfall of harlot Rome that reverberates from John's revelation of the end of time.

What does this say to our urban churches as they remain—sometimes glorious and sometimes grubby—in the midst of a shrinking tax base, declining capital concentrations, and continuing curtailment of services to the poor and the old and the urban-impacted whom the environing society has declared its rejects and its "losers?" It calls attention to what these churches too often are—frail, feeble, confused, and ambiguous—and also to what these churches are trying to be: colonies of hope and meaning for people who have great difficulty finding either. In a time when so many have lost hope that either the city or the church can have value or meaning and have, instead, "turned east"—or north, south, west—in search of new religious esoterica or revivalism, the *urban ministry* is charged with the task of raising and pressing the question of the city—holding up the vision on the one hand and challenging the reality on the

45

other.

The starting point of "urban ministry" is the recognition of "presence:" the deep realization that we are called to be present IN the city, but also present TO the city. This realization involves us in difficult and trying choices, not only as they relate to where we place our Unitarian-Universalist dollars but also where we place our personal involvement and our priorities. It means being responsible to the agendas of the entrapped and oppressed who lack power to exercise control over their lives or the life of their communities.

Who are these people? Where are they? Why do they lack power? Who holds the power that serves to maintain them in misery? Do they exist in our communities and in our churches? If "yes," what have we done to alleviate or change their situation for the better? If "no," what have we done to identify and deal with the structures that prevent them from being among us or that encourage their "invisibility" in our midst? As we define them, how do they "define" us?

These are not questions to be asked only of churches and congregations located within our few isolated urban parishes, but in the many sub-urban, ex-urban and rural settings as well. From these questions, and answers to them, could flow a renewing decision to engage the environing society—in a dialogue that will identify and test interests and stakes for changing the condition of the underclass.

Urban ministry within our Unitarian Universalist structure is being pursued wherever such questions are seriously asked and pondered. Our Unitarian Universalist Service Committee was engaged in urban ministry as it pursued the cause of prison reform and demanded a moratorium on prison construction. The Rev. Jack Mendelsohn's leadership of a Chicago coalition of churches calling for greater accountability from and control over that city's police is an example of "urban ministry." The work of our Boston based Benevolent Fraternity of Unitarian Universalist churches encouraging its ministers to take active roles in demanding more effective police response to racist attacks upon

Boston citizens is "urban ministry." The creation of a coalition of concerned church people from several congregations who commit themselves to study and then demand that a local bank make itself accountable to them for its continued dealings with the racist government of South Africa is an example of "urban ministry." Wherever the powers that be are being named and tested in the cause of, and in solidarity with those without power, urban ministry is being pursued.

Each of these examples of "urban ministry" rests upon and, in some measure, is the result of a prior decision: the decision to stop being ineffectual. Our efforts in any or all of the projects which we undertake may come to naught—that is the risk we run—but, at least, our defeats will not be the result of our own predisposition.

What might we undertake that would enhance and facilitate "urban ministry?" We might require that a precondition for full ministerial fellowship in our association include a period of time serving a church affected by the urban condition or placed in an association dealing with urban problems. One object of such an experience being that when the ministerial candidates are called to pulpits of suburban churches, they would be in a position to do more than reinforce the fears and fantasies of their congregations as relate to the urban scene, and they could encourage their people to be involved in some meaningful way with the concerns of that under-class which populates our cities.

Earlier in this essay I quoted Gibson Winter's statement that the so-called "urban crisis is less a crisis than a degenerative disease which is reaching a critical stage." Winter points out that because of the nature of the disease, crisis measures will be of little help. He says, "We are dealing with fundamental structures and values of the society—structures which we can only change through generations of effort."

Because we Americans tend to be immediate and non-historical in responding to social situations, the very idea that entire generations will be involved if our urban situation is to be salvaged seems in itself apocalyptic. Yet what better indication of the need of the church—the one institution in our society which has manifested its staying power and resourcefulness—to remind us of what is transient and what is permanent; remind us by its continued presence in our urban areas of the truth and challenge in the words of Gwendolyn Brooks:

*We are each other's harvest.*
*We are each other's magnitude and bond.*

## NOTES

1  From "The Children's Puzzle: A Study of Children's Services in Massachusetts," Commonwealth of Massachusetts Publication, 1977.

2. Sam Bass Warner, *The Urban Wilderness: A History of the American City.* Harper & Row, 1972, p. 266.

3. Catherine L. Carpenter, unpublished ms., 1975.

4. Robert L. Heilbroner, "Marx Now," *New York Review of Books,* Vol. XXV. No. 11 (1978).

5. Max Stackhouse, "The City as Possibility," *Journal of Current Social Issues,* Winter 1972-73.

6. Quoted from testimony included in *The Episcopal Church in the Urban Crisis: 1978-1988.* A Draft Document, prepared by Joseph A. Pelham for The Urban Bishops' Coalition.

7. James Luther Adams, *On Being Human Religiously.* Beacon Press, 1976, p. 67.

8. "The City, Being In It and Being Of It," Address by The Rev. Jack Mendelsohn at Conference of Center City Churches, Philadelphia, Oct. 1972.

# 3

# ...IN THE CITY

# WHOSE CITY IS IT ANYWAY?

Adapted from a Sermon at Arlington Street Church
Boston, MA 1982

*Behold, the Lord was standing beside a wall built
with a plumb line, with a plumb line in his hand. And
the Lord said to me, "Amos, what do you see?" And I
said, "A plumb line." Then the Lord said, "Behold, I
am setting a plumb line in the midst of my people
Israel; I will never again pass by them; the high places
of Isaac shall be made desolate, and the sanctuaries
of Israel shall be laid waste, and I shall rise against the
house of Jeroboam with the sword."*

*Then Amaziah, the priest of Bethel went to Jero-
boam, king of Israel, saying, "Amos has conspired
against you in the midst of the house of Israel; the land
is not able to bear all his words. For thus Amos has
said, 'Jeroboam shall die by the sword, and Israel
must go into exile away from his land.'"*

*And Amaziah said to Amos, "O seer, go, flee away
to the land of Judah, and eat bread there, and prophesy there; but never again prophesy at Bethel, for it
is the king's sanctuary, and it is a temple of the
kingdom."*

*Then Amos answered Amaziah, "I am no prophet,
nor a prophet's son; but I am a herdsman, and a
dresser of sycamore trees, and the Lord took me from
following the flock, and the Lord said to me, 'Go,
prophesy to my people Israel.'"*

- Amos 7:15-25

Twenty-four hundred years ago the Greek playwright
Euripides advised his Hellenic audience, "The first requisite
of happiness is that a person be born in a famous city."

The Greeks took their cities very seriously. Today, identification with a famous city is still a source of self-esteem.

My Presbyterian colleague, The Reverend Joe Williamson, tells a story of two visitors to his summer home on Cape Breton Island. The young couple was on a clam-digging expedition and asked if Joe was a year-round resident of the island. On learning that he was from Boston, the couple said how nice it was to meet a neighbor so far north. Joe inquired where in Boston they were from. It turned out that they were not from Boston, or from a Boston suburb, nor, indeed, from a Boston exurb. They were from Southern New Hampshire! But they still identified themselves with a great city. It was one component of their own self-esteem.

The Greeks used to compete with each other as to which of their cities could construct the most elaborate embellishment or stage the most extravagant display. Again it would appear that there are parallels between the Greeks' attitudes towards their urban centers and the recent shift in our attitudes toward ours. Fifteen years ago the city was the court of last resort. As the song advised, "When you're alone and life is making you lonely, you can always GO DOWNTOWN."

But in the intervening years this attitude seems to have reversed itself. *The Saturday Review* published a story on how the American metropolis has become one of the hottest commodities in marketing. The article was titled, "Love Thy City." It reported that cities across the country are about the business of constructing ever more elaborate embellishments and staging ever more extravagant displays— an Astrodome here, a hotel to rival the pyramids there.

The frightening thing which the article calls attention to is how our cities are becoming dominated by a marketing mentality. This means that the thinking of the cities' leadership, its decision-makers, has shifted from a concern about what is *Good* for the city to a concern about what will help to *Sell* the city.

"Selling the city" is a way of bringing in dollars to make it

52

more attractive and, presumably, more livable. I am not going to argue against attempts to upgrade our urban environments. They are necessary and do, indeed, serve a socially desirable purpose. But once we move beyond such generalities and begin to consider specifics, the short-sighted and basically anti-human aspects of the marketing mentality become apparent.

The urban areas that are getting the face-lifts are those which are attractive to and cater to people with money, and have the potential of attracting more affluent people. People with money are the people who are attractive to advertisers, so places where these people gather are places that the advertising media tend to focus on. The marketing mentality has dictated that public money be poured into Boston's upscale, trendy Quincy Market, while the nationally notorious Columbia Point Housing Development was left to sink into Boston Harbor for decades until a plan to attract "the moneyed" was devised for the area. It does not end there. The marketing mentality identifies each one of us as a consumer and, only secondarily, if at all, as a citizen. It follows, therefore, that money is made available to gratify the desires of consumers who can pay for services and commodities rather than to provide services to those who cannot. Banks and financial institutions applaud the spread of urban gentrification, while slum areas continue to be "red-lined."

In his majestic study, *The City in History*, Lewis Mumford points out that by the Fourth Century B.C. (which was the period of Greek Urban expansion), the Athenians insisted on spending their money on public games and festivals. Says Mumford, "They were too enamored of their habitual excitements and distractions—their sports, their games and shows, and their new interest in fine cooking—to be willing to confront the life and death realities that called for sacrifice." Sounds familiar! Any resident of a city whose team carries its name into a playoff, a world series, or a superbowl can readily apply Mumford's observation to his and her hometown.

And regarding the increased interest in fine cuisine, we can all identify with the culinary blitz that is one of the hallmarks of the "new" Boston, San Francisco, Philadelphia... (Lest you think I am adopting a holier than thou attidude toward gourmet dining, just invite me to join you for lunch at Boston's Locke Obers or any exclusive eatery.)

Yet, for all our fine restaurants, entertainments, and public proclamations that Boston, Washington, New York, Seattle, Chicago...is a very livable city, we need to remind ourselves that each one is a livable city only for those whose faces are white and whose pockets have green.

*The Boston Globe* published a story about how few black people attend Red Sox games at Fenway Park. Is it because black people are culturally unable to relate to baseball, as the Red Sox management would like us to believe, or is it that the black people who do risk venturing into Fenway Park fear for their personal safety (as one after another black person who was interviewed testified).

And it is not only in the vicinity of Fenway Park that a person of color might feel threatened. There is a map of Boston on the wall of the office of the Community Disorders Unit at Boston Police headquarters studded with map-tacks marking sites of violent attacks on Boston citizens. Since I was one of the people at whose urging this particular police unit was established, I have retained a keen interest in its progress and its implicit testimony to the truth that people of color are not as safe to move about freely in this city as white people. Undoubtedly the same is true of other U.S. cities, beyond the confines of segregated black ghettos.

Boston is certainly a livable city if you are affluent. But the economic development of this city and the impact upon the less affluent have been disastrous. Between the movement of wealthy people into Boston and the expansion of the universities and other institutions, poor people and people of moderate means are increasingly being forced either to leave intown residential areas or to pay inordinate amounts of their income in rent. (Purchase of property for low to moderate income families is no longer an option.)

If we accept the image of ourselves as consumers and The city as a consumable—as Big Mac—then none of the foregoing is relevant, and the only question we need to ask is how can we get the most "buzz for our bucks." But if we prefer the self-image of citizen rather than consumer, then the true condition of our inner city neighbor becomes a matter of paramount significance for us.

Some time ago, poet John Ciardi published a critical piece about Emily Dickinson, the so-called "Belle of Amherst" who wrote those splendid spare verses that exposed reality. Ciardi said that when Dickinson finished a poem, her first concern was "Did I tell it true?" and not "Can I sell it to Hallmark?" That's the difference between the citizen mentality and the consumer marketing mentality.

The concern for "telling it true" is at the center of the conflict between Amos and Amaziah, the priest of Bethel and mouthpiece for King Jeroboam. The occasion is Amos' vision of the plumb line which he sees God holding against a sagging wall. Amos sees it, but doesn't speak. Why not? Scholarly opinion says that in that historic period (around 800 BCE) there was a generally recognized division between what people exercised control over and what God controlled. Such seasonal occurrences as a famine or a drought—were beyond the power of human effort to control, so one could turn to God and do a bit of plea bargaining. But a wall was different. A wall was the product of human labor. If a wall buckles, for whatever reason, its deviation is inexorably marked by the plumb line. From the verdict of the plumb line there is no appeal. So Amos silently accepts the finality of the judgement.

The wall is a good urban image. Cities are made of walls. The city is the creation of human labor and its problems demand human confrontation and human solution.

The full impact of Amos' vision is conveyed by the priest Amaziah who calls Amos a traitor. Note that Amos is accused not because of his message (he "tells it true") but because "the land is not able to bear his words." Amaziah doesn't question Amos' veracity, but rather the threatening impact of his message upon the land.

Several years ago Boston was witness to an Amaziah-Amos confrontation. It occurred (as such confrontations invariably occur) in the context of a struggle for the office of Mayor of the city. A black state representative (Mel King) challenged the white mayoral imcumbent (Kevin White) to look at the plumb line. White retreated from King's challenge to address the issues of racism, sexism, housing and transportation that strangle the city. White retreated.

Dr. Erna Ballantyne Bryant, who was President of the Black Ecumenical Commission, reminded me of the ancient Greek legend about the great peril that ships encountered when they had to sail the straits of Scylla and Charybdis. Not only were they in danger because of proximity to rocks, the danger was multiplied by songs of the Sirens luring the sailors to their deaths. Two famous sailors made it through those perilous straits, each adopting a different tactic for dealing with the threat. Ulysses ordered the sailors' ears to be plugged with wax so they wouldn't hear the Sirens' songs then lashed them to the mast as an extra precautionary measure.

The second sailor adopted a very different method of dealing with the peril. Orpheus ordered his sailors to play their own musical instruments and to play such sweet music that they would not be enticed by the Siren song.

The two options from this legend are open to us. The Ulysses option is the option of illusion and self-doubt. Plugging one's ears and closing one's eyes won't make the Sirens or the rocks go away. The Orpheus option is the option of realism and communal faith. The Orpheus option suggests that we confront life and use our own resources in dealing with it. In the Orpheus combo each sailor played his own instrument, but they played together.

The Mayor of Boston represented the Ulysses option; the State Representative (concerned with returning power to people and creating a climate for significant social change) captured the flavor of Orpheus' method of surviving the peril. The Mayor won out—for that time and place. But there are "sailors" among us piping together today in cities across our nation, trying to provide a music that awakens a spiritual depth and social commitment within us.

Politics is caring about people, caring about the quality of our common life. But for this care to have substance and form, we must, in Lewis Mumford's words, "be willing to confront the life and death realities that call for sacrifice."

If we seek new values in the city, we will add new values to the city. Our collective resolve to do what each of us can do about those problems has the power to bring these values to full reality. The city belongs to all of us, and we share responsibility for its nurture. Remember Jesse Jackson's great litany for power:

> *"If you can conceive it and believe it, you can achieve it. It's not your aptitude, but your attitude that determines your altitude with a little fortitude. We are called, not to be servile, but to be of service - for service is power!"*

Whose city is it? Yours and mine. Let us be about its rightful role.

# SO WHERE'S
# THE "COMMON GROUND"?

Adapted from a Sermon at
Arlington Street Church
Boston, MA 1985

Ecclesiastes—that mordant observer of the human condition—made the sour remark that "of the making of books there is no end." I could go Ecclesiastes one better. Of the making of books *about Boston* there is no end. I do not believe there ever was an American city that has been so thoroughly poked and prodded, analyzed and moralized about, as has the "city upon a hill." Who needs another book about Boston? That was my attitude as I approached Anthony Lukas's huge volume entitled *Common Ground*. Having read the book I can only answer my question by saying, "I do, you do, in fact all Americans need *this* book about Boston."

*Common Ground* is about Boston and the desegregation of its de-facto segregated public school system. It spans the decade from 1968 to 1978 (the decade which began ominously with the assassination of Martin Luther King, Jr.). The story of Boston's struggle with desegregation is told as it impacted on the lives of three Boston families, all of whom had children in the Boston school system. The Twymons are a large black family with roots in both the rural South and in Boston's long standing black community. The Twymon family is headed by Rachel Twymon, a single parent who lived for most of this period in a rent-assisted housing development on Columbus Avenue in Boston's South End section. The McGoffs are an equally large family, all of Irish American lineage, headed by the recently widowed Alice McGoff, who live in the Bunker Hill housing project in ethnically insulated Charlestown.

Although much of the book is devoted to both the Twymons and the McGuffs, it is really the third family that
frames the story and provides its main focus. *Common
Ground* centers around the story of Joan and Colin Diver, a
well-educated, professional couple of suburban White
Anglo-Saxon Protestant (WASP) background, who live in a
renovated townhouse in the South End of Boston. The
stories of the Divers, the McGoffs and the Twymons are
interlaced with character studies of principal players in the
desegregation scenario such as segregation activist Louise
Day Hicks; Judge Arthur Garrity, who produced the court
order mandating integration of the school system, the
Roman Catholic Archdiocese's Humberto Cardinal Madie-
ros; Thomas Winship, publisher of the *Boston Globe*; and
the ever-resilient ex-Boston Mayor, Kevin White, who (as
Lukas reminds us) was, "for one brief shining moment"
George McGovern's choice for running mate on the 1972
Democratic ticket.

But *Common Ground* is not a piece of social science. It is
the story of three Boston families caught up in a profound
social dilemma. As Lukas himself says: "The families at the
center of my story were not selected as statistical averages
or norms. On the contrary, I was drawn to them by a special
intensity and engagement with life, which made them stand
out from their social context." Several commentators have
seen Lukas's focus on individual lives as a problem. They
say it is all very well to give us the minutia of people's day to
day existence, but how does one generalize from the indiv-
ual case? How do we fathom or ferret out the larger meanings of the material? I did not find this problemmatic.

By telling the stories of these individuals, Lukas invites the
reader to compare and contrast—to hold our individual
experience against (or alongside of) the experiences of the
McGoffs, the Twymons, the Divers. And it works. Those
who know the social scenes, the physical surroundings,
know that they are "the real thing." Yes, Columbus Avenue
does look and feel like the book's descriptions...yes, that is
exactly the way street crime happens...yes, that is how

so and so would react in that kind of situation.

I personally know little about Charlestown where the McGoffs live, so I am prepared to take what Lukas, and others I have spoken with, says about that community on face value. The Twymons and the Divers both live in the South End. That fact alone should be sufficient for churches such as Arlington Street Church (where I ministered from 1976 to 1987), King's Chapel, First and Second Church, Community Church, and denominational headquarters to pay close attention. They all stand within walking distance of Boston's South End.

While Boston's school desegregation was headline news during a decade (1968 to 1978), an equally fateful drama was beginning in Boston's South End. We identify that drama by the description "Gentrification." Beginning in the 1960s and picking up steam during the 1970s, "gentrification" refashioned the South End. To his great credit, author Anthony Lukas shows sympathy for both "sides" in the process of profound urban change. He is sympathetic with those who came into the South End with money and vision—attracted by the Victorian ambiance of those who had originally built the district during the 19th Century. And he is sympathetic to the plight of those who were displaced—people who lived there simply because they needed decent, affordable housing near mass transit, public hospitals, health clinics, and work.

During the period of the book's focus, the South End was the most integrated area of Boston. There still exists a mythology about the South End which proclaims it (at least at that time) as an area where all people, classes, races, lived—if not in total harmony—at least in a creative (if occasionally tense) relationship. The fact is that the South End *was* an open, inclusive, fluid, ready for definition area of Boston. That was its virtue.

In those years it seemed possible to build a new kind of community in the South End—without the kind of housing deterioration, high street crime, bad public image that drive people away from urban neighborhoods in what has been characterized as "white flight". But the much hoped-for "new South End" never quite came together. The main reason why the dream faded can be summed up in two words: "housing market." Property prices went beyond where the middle could hold. The healthy diversity of race, class, ethnic group could not be sustained. The "new South End," this urban dream of harmonious racial and economic diversity was symbolized in the South End's Bancroft Public School. This long desegregated school was the embodiment of both the white, well-educated, upper middle class values (reflecting the attitudes of the new South Enders) and the dream of quality education for black and Latino children (as dreamed by their parents living in projects, low income rentals, and subsidized housing units). The school was thrown into disarray by the desegregation process. Today the Bancroft Public School is a new luxury condominium complex.

Of the three families whose lives frame the account of *Common Ground*, the story of Joan and Colin Diver is the story with which white liberals will most readily identify. The Divers are "Yuppies." (I do not intend that identification as a pejorative term.) The Divers are young professionals who moved into the urban scene bringing with them energy, intelligence, optimism and quantities of good will. They're liberals, Lord love 'em, and they want to change the city, to make it a better place for ALL of its people. They moved into the South End at the sacrifice of higher potential income and potential comfort. They moved into an aging neighborhood willingly, and enthusiastically threw themselves into the midst of its problems.

The Diver's story is a Pilgrim's Progress—but without a happy ending. They discovered that the urban problems are more entrenched, more complicated, more intractable than their own physical, psychological, moral reserves of strength and purpose could deal with. In 1976 the Divers reluctantly sold the brick row house in the South End and moved to the fashionable suburb of Newton. In the personage of the Divers we see the bright hopes of the 1960s and the 1970s turn into the bitter ashes of the 1980s. They will not let themselves care that deeply again. And there are many like them.

As I read *Common Ground*, I could not help but reflect on the fact that nowhere in this 800 page book is any Boston Unitarian Universalist church or organization even mentioned in passing. Here is Boston, racked and convulsed by a great social issue. Here are more than half a dozen liberal church congregations within the metropolitan area and the headquarters of a continent-wide liberal religious association of churches. We pride ourselves on our willingness to grapple with social issues. Yet, for all the contact between us and the social upheaval of that period, we might just as well have been located in a remote suburb.

If Joan and Colin Diver had been members of a local Unitarian Unversalist church during that period, would it have made a difference in their lives and in their decision to stay or leave Boston? If members of any of the several Unitarian-Universalist communities had organized themselves into an effective peace-keeping cadre to confront and disarm such militant, anti-social, disruptive forces as the organization called ROAR (Restore Our Alienated Rights), would that have made a difference? If I or the collective leadership of Arlington Street Church had taken it upon ourselves to reach out to the leadership of local congregations in the South End such as the Union United Methodist Church (where Rachel Twymon was deeply involved), would we have been able to serve as a bridge of communication between the embattled white South End liberals like the Divers and the struggling, beleaguered black community of this city?

Because I am acquainted with the internal travail that this community was experiencing during the early years of the 1970s (the period of the book's focus), I realize that there simply was not the energy to grapple with some of the "what ifs" I have mentioned. And it certainly is not my intention to engage in a useless exercise of head-shaking. But energy has *returned* to the Arlington Street Church, and to other

62

Unitarian Universalist communities. Now it is appropriate to look at ourselves—as urban churches—in the city of Boston or across America in any city still desperately seeking *common ground*. The mission of an urban church: to organize and empower people to take control of their lives and their circumstances; to unify and strengthen the personhood of each individual; to strengthen our denomination and its commitment to urban ministry; to seek strategies and answers by posing discerning questions and moving to supportive action.

The "Common Ground" is the ground upon which we stand—together. Our task is to extend that common ground in order to provide all persons with cities fit for human habitation, human community, human reformation and renewal.

# THE ASSASSINATION
## OF A CITY'S SOUL

If you are 35 years old or older, you probably remember precisely where you were and what you were doing when you heard the news that President John Kennedy had been assassinated in Dallas. Indeed, we have had ample opportunity to reflect upon that tragedy over the years.

The twenty-fifth anniversary of that grim event occasioned a media blitz focusing on the tragedy in Dallas and upstaging another tragedy. That "other" tragedy not only has special meaning for San Francisco but has cultural and national implications as well. I refer to the fact that 1988 marked the tenth anniversary of the assassinations of San Francisco City Supervisor Harvey Milk and San Francisco Mayor George Moscone, by former City Supervisor Dan White.

If you lived in San Francisco ten years ago, you assuredly remember where you were and what you were doing when you heard that Mayor Moscone and Supervisor Milk had been shot at City Hall. Your memories of that tragic moment are probably sharp and focused.

I confess that I have no such memory. Ten years ago I lived in Boston, and although the news of the assassinations impacted upon me, that impact was overshadowed by the inconceivable disaster which had occurred at Jonestown, Guyana only nine days earlier. However, I have come to conclude that the shootings of George Moscone and Harvey Milk by Dan White have greater historical and cultural significance today, for the city of San Francisco and for our American society, than "Jonestown"—despite the grisly perversion that word has come to imply.

"Jonestown" was and remains a grotesque and horrendous aberration, a mind-boggling madness. By contrast, the double murder at City Hall was a prophetic indicator of the

64

American fear of the 1980s, a fear which could be summed up as a fear of moral and social anarchy.

Here, briefly, are the facts. On November 27, 1978, Mayor George Moscone and Supervisor Harvey Milk were shot to death at City Hall by Dan White, ex-high school athlete, ex-Viet Nam veteran, ex-policeman, ex-fireman, ex-City Supervisor. Dan White thought he had a grievance. He had resigned from the San Francisco Board of Supervisors and then asked for his job back. But Mayor Moscone, with Supervisor Milk's concurrence, had decided to appoint someone else to that position.

White was a working-class Roman Catholic conservative, George Moscone was a liberal pragmatist and Harvey Milk was the first openly gay person ever elected to public office in the United States of America.

Although Dan White admitted the killings, a friendly jury convicted him not of murder but of voluntary manslaughter; and he was released from prison after serving less than five years of a seven-year sentence.

In October 1985, Dan White committed suicide (which could be inferred as a last gesture of agreement that the sentence had been too light, or as corroboration of the defense counsel's theory that White was a victim of severe depression.) In either case, the central questions remain: Why did Dan White commit the murders, and why did he get off so lightly? My answer to these questions is that Dan White and his friendly jury did what they did for exactly the same reasons. They were affected and afflicted with the 1980s American fear of moral and social anarchy.

The fundamental fact of American life in the 1980s is that the revolution of the 1960s was both a failure and a success. Consider first the failure.

The "hippies" are history. The "flower children" have long since wilted. Mind-altering drugs, hailed in the 1960s as panaceas, have turned out to be personal and social poisons. Upscale consumerism has become even more blatantly self-indulgent, as anyone walking through nationwide shopping malls (some of which boast circular escalators and splashing fountains as symbols of civilization's advance) can testify. On the basis of such evidence, many people have concluded that the revolution of the 1960s was a failure. But that is only half of the story.

One has to admit that there *has* been a revolution in the past decades, and that revolution has been in the area of personal behavior. All sorts of social controls, controls by consensus, and controls by complusion, have been loosened or totally abandoned in the last few years. Many things which were once unthinkable have become possible, do-able, commonplace. In a number of ways, the national id seems to have replaced the national superego.

Some of these changes, especially in the codes of sexual and gender discrimination, have brought liberation to many. But as codes and values and laws lose their power, people are left feeling bewildered, unprotected, deserted, undermined, and yes, even betrayed.

For a great many people in our society, the most flagrant symbol of frightening change resulting from the abandonment of social controls has been the public emergence of the homosexual subculture. What was once considered to be unspeakable degeneracy, perversion, unnatural vice, is now a matter of pride, to be openly claimed and acknowledged. It is no coincidence that San Francisco, reputedly the gay capital of America, is where ex-Supervisor Dan White, heterosexual, conservative, Roman Catholic, shot and killed the gay City Supervisor, and San Francisco's gay-protecting Mayor. The rounds fired into the bodies of Mayor Moscone and Supervisor Milk were meant to kill more than the two men. The intention was nothing less than the assassination of the city's liberal soul.

There is no question that the killings of George Moscone and Harvey Milk were acts of homophobia. There is also no question that the absurdly light sentence which the jury handed down to Dan White was an endorsement of homophobia. The conclusion which can and should be drawn from these facts is that there is an underlying feeling in our society to this day that Dan White stood for what is right in America, and that Moscone and Milk symbolized the decay of our society.

Dan White was a pathological killer. But I think it is important to remember that pathological persons are generally just like the rest of us—only more so. The fear that drove Dan White was shared and is shared today, in some measure, by the jury that convicted him of voluntary manslaughter and by the society from which that jury was selected. Our society. Us. The fear that drove him is shared by vast numbers of our countrymen and country women.

In a recent article entitled, "The New Emphasis on Teaching of Values," the author, who is president of the National Education Association, is quoted as saying, "People are afraid that the moral fiber of their country is falling apart." The current AIDS epidemic and the drug panic both partake of this great and overriding fear. Note that a recent Gallup poll cited drugs as the number one American concern in this age of political, nuclear, and environmental worldwide annihilation.

This fear has made heroes out of Rambo and Dirty Harry, this fear elected Ronald Reagan twice to the Presidency of this country, this fear boosted George Bush into the Oval Office. In its pervasiveness, this fear rivals the changes in values and the changes in behavior to which it is a reaction. We are all its victims.

Unitarian Universalists, religious liberals, assembled under the banner of freedom, reason, and tolerance, were the subject of a 1987 survey carried out at the urging of the denominatinal Office of Gay Affairs. The survey revealed a startling high incidence of homophobia in the enlightened ranks of Unitarian Universalist churches. So we religious liberals must begin by admitting to homophobia within ourselves or our communities, and acknowledging that homophobia reflects a fear that those who are, for the most part straight, white and middle class, are losing control of the U.S. society.

It is in the oldest and most time-honored of religious traditions that confession and the acknowledgement of one's shortcomings open the door to healing and restoration. On the 10th anniversary (as on each anniversary of the grim event) a candlelight march for Milk and Moscone moved through San Francisco to the steps of City Hall. No one expected a march to heal a trauma as deep as the assassinations had caused, particularly since they cut directly to a fundamental division in the city of San Francisco. Cities, too, take time to heal, and to process their grief. But the citywide candlelight march has been a good symbolic beginning.

For the longer term, I urge a deeper regard for the tragedy of AIDS as it afflicts people in San Francisco, across our nation and around the world. If we might achieve some deep internalization of feeling for how AIDS affects those who suffer, then we might allow our feelings to move forward to reconciliation of the disunions and the divisions between and among people and groups of people.

Thinking about instruments which serve to produce reconciliation, I recall the Viet Nam memorial in Washington, D.C., a masterpiece of a grieving mechanism that is serving to heal our nation. To visit the memorial, to descend into that valley of death, the names of the fallen rising gradually above your head, is to experience immersion in grief and mourning. The memorial gives permission to vent a national grief stored up for the 59,000 men and women killed in that faraway war.

By the end of 1988 more than 48,000 people, nearly three quarters of the number killed in Viet Nam, have fallen in the AIDS war. And there still is no end to this war in sight. We need actual and symbolic means of alleviating our grief, our confusion, our sense of loss. The AIDS Quilt, representing the Names Project, mammoth and simultaneously deeply personal, attempts to fulfill that need, releasing a deep caring and sharing attitude for the victims and for the aggrieved in our society. But we need more.

We need to re-examine our hearts, our lives, our social attitudes and our social involvements. We need to make an inventory of our fears as they relate to the American malaise of the 1980s. Let us be clear with ourselves and with each other about the nature and content of our fear: Are we afraid of "social anarchy" or of losing control of a society in which heterosexually oriented white men have long dominated? And finally, let us remember that love and caring break through the most rigid situations to bring their gifts of reconciliation, liberation, and peace as we confront the valleys of fear and loss together.

# AFRAIDS

When I was in high school, my assigned reading list included Edgar Allan Poe's thriller, *The Masque of the Red Death*. I enjoyed it as an imaginative horror story. Only later did I come to appreciate it as a parable. Here is the story in synopsis. Royalty and courtesans of France, isolated and insulated by their wealth and privilege from the ravages of the Bubonic Plague (the Red Death) retreat to the country-side, there to entertain themselves until the unpleasantness subsides. They plan a "mask," what we would call a costume party. In the course of the festivities, Red Death itself appears in their midst with shocking and horrific force testifying to the adage that "you can run but you can't hide."

AIDS (Acquired Immune Deficiency Syndrome) and ARC (AIDS-Related Complex) are moving among us. The Reverend Mark DeWolfe, Unitarian Universalist minister, was diagnosed as having contracted AIDS in 1986. Mark died in July, 1988, while serving his first Unitarian-Universalist congregation in Ontario, Canada, where he was ordained in 1982. To my knowledge, Mark is the first Unitarian Universalist minister actively serving one of our churches to be diagnosed as having AIDS. He was my colleague. He could have been my son. He is our brother. With Mark's diagnosis AIDS "appeared" in *our* midst. AIDS is moving among *us*.

We can run from this news. We can say that Mark was gay and that AIDS is a gay disease, discounting the fact that a high percentage of persons contracting AIDS are not gay but are I.V. drug users. We can say that Mark wasn't careful, discounting the fact that no degree of care or caution helps the hemophiliac who acquires AIDS because of tainted blood. We can engage ourselves in blaming the victim while ignoring the fact that AIDS is not a gay issue. It is a public health issue. AIDS is moving among us. We can run but we can't hide. And we are afraid.

At a 1986 conference on AIDS convened by the Episcopal Church in New England, one of the clergy brought in a copy of the *New York Times* which carried a report of a dialogue between President Ronald Reagan and Secretary of State George Schultz. Their topic was Moammar Quadaffi, Libya's leader and the Reagan administration's bete noire. According to the report, Schultz suggested that Quadaffi be invited to spend time in San Francisco in the expectation that there he would stand a good chance of acquiring AIDS.

The clergy attending the conference were appalled that AIDS should be a topic of homophobic banter by persons of such authority. A letter of protest was drafted. However, upon its presentation to the group several voices rose against sending it in the name of the conference, and some attendees said they would refuse to sign for fear of revealing their presence at the conference. They feared negative repercussions if their attendance at an AIDS conference were to become public knowledge.

AIDS is a guilt-by-association disease. To attend a conference on AIDS and AIDS-Related Complex (ARC) is to court suspicion. It was not so long ago (during the Joe McCarthy era when that senator from Wisconsin was running roughshod over the U.S. Constitution) that the label "homosexual" was sufficient to provoke public hysteria.

Homophobia is still "alive and well" even in our liberal and enlightened Unitarian Universalist churches and fellowships. We still live in a period when participation in a conference on AIDS is cause for suspicion and negative judgment about one's life and one's associations.

AIDS is moving among us. We feel threatened—if not by AIDS then by the negative whispers, asides, innuendoes that crowd around AIDS. We risk catching "AFRAIDS."

"AFRAIDS" is also a public health issue. It strikes directly at the public's mental health and welfare systems. Everyone is in the "high risk " group. It is transmitted by the public media and is highly contagious.

You come home from work early one day and turn on the

TV just in time to watch one of those ten-second news breaks. There is the anchorman. He is popular. His face is familiar. You trust him. But on this day he looks anxious. He says, "Tragic news. Elementary school food handler has died of AIDS. Details at six."

If you would have found such a news break unsettling, you have contracted "Afraids." A 1986 newscast did report such a story. Listeners confessed to having visions of that AIDS sufferer (lesions and sores in full view, busily cutting up carrot sticks that children would soon consume). The 6 p.m. news reported that, indeed, an elementary school food handler *had* died of AIDS. However, she had retired from food preparation in the school system ten years earlier, and had acquired AIDS because she had recently received a transfusion of tainted blood.

How we get information about AIDS and ARC is important for dealing with our "Afraids." The important fact that the 70-year-old woman had not been employed by the school system for ten years, had been omitted from the news break. The story was broadcast in June 1986 in New York City in precisely the manner that I have described. The purpose was not to provide sound information, but to exploit the public's fear for the sake of a higher percentage of the viewing audience. Millions of Americans recieve all their information about the world from TV newscasts and from ten-second spot announcements. Thus the media's irresponsible coverage fans a climate of hysteria surrounding the topic of AIDS. The source of information is as important as the information itself. Clear, medically accurate information is as crucial in dealing with "Afraids" as with AIDS.

In addition to information free from media distortion, we need a safe and secure climate in which the information we receive can be processed openly and honestly. We need a climate of welcome that accepts not only those who suffer from AIDS but also those who suffer from "Afraids." A place where the recipient of scare news, the confused, the uncertain, and, yes, the homophobic can come with their questions and their concerns. Is the homophobic's attitude repellent? Yes. Are her/his perspectives distorted? Probably. But unless and until we succeed in creating atmospheres where we can come together, the "Afraids" plague will continue to ravage our communities.

One congregation in New York City, the All Souls Unitarian Universalist Church, accepted the challenge to confront "Afraids" and created just such a community. While continuing to minister actively to those afflicted with AIDS, it launched a bold and imaginative campaign against "Afraids" by placing billboard notices in New York subway cars calling attention to its AIDS ministry and inviting anyone with questions concerning AIDS to contact All Souls Unitarian Universalist Church.

All Souls in New York is not a church which the average New Yorker associated with street ministry to the poor or the oppressed. All Souls is not a Unitarian Universalist version of The Catholic Worker or St. Marks on the Bowery. All Souls is located on the very fashionable upper East Side. It is associated with style, affluence, social position. That it would lend its considerable prestige to combat "Afraids" in such a bold and direct way as public connection with AIDS is worthy of respect, admiration, and emulation.

The AIDS advisory panel of the Unitarian Universalist Association has published a book of activities and programs that churches around the country provide. We do well to remember such initiatives when we are told that only the religious right is speaking out on the issue with statements that link AIDS with prostitution or that it is "God's way of clearing out useless people."

Despite various responses to the contrary, "Afraids" has occasioned attacks upon even mild and seemingly irreproachable initiatives. A 1987 worship service was organized to remember all who suffer from AIDS or ARC. The service, presided over by New York Bishop Paul Moore, was scurrilously attacked by columnist William Buckley. In his syndicated column Buckley wrote, "Is Bishop Moore planning a memorial for Stalin and his henchmen; another for those who die of syphilis; another for those who O.D. on cocaine? What is really missing from the Bishop and from fellow travelers in this brand of groundless compassion is any consideration of this: some AIDS sufferers would rather contaminate other people, causing them to die a miserable death, than to control their own perverse appetites."

I set William Buckley's mean-spirited, homophobic diatribe over against the words of a young man, Don Perrin by name, who addressed an AIDS conference in a suit that was three sizes too big for him. His face was sallow and gaunt. His hair sparse. His eyes deep in their sockets. He told us that three years previously he discovered he had AIDS. A hemophiliac, Don Perrin received blood that harbored the disease. He spoke first of his anger, specifically his anger directed at the gay community which, he believed, had been responsible for providing the tainted blood in the first place. As the experience of the disease widened and deepened, Don Perrin discovered his attitude had changed. He experienced the stigma that all who suffer from AIDS experience: The dentist who refuses to perform oral surgery. The ambulance driver who refuses to pick up the accident victim. The schoolchildren who refuse to associate with your children because you or they have AIDS. Mr. Perrin's attitude changed. From anger and aloofness, he moved to identification and solidarity. He described his new sense of community with all AIDS sufferers. He used the phrase, "soldiers in a trench."

By 1988, 43,000 had died of AIDS. As of September 1989 the figure of U.S. AIDS related deaths had risen to 64,849 according to one public report*. New AIDS and ARC cases are diagnosed every day. Medical research holds promise of AIDS drug management as a chronic disease. Few can afford such management. In a capitalist society lacking a national health care system, the AIDS sequelae born of separatist mentality fuels "Afraids" all the more.

AIDS and AFRAIDS move among us. We have a choice. We can identify with William Buckley and the disdainful French nobility. Or we can choose to hunker down in that trench with Don Perrin, The Rev. Mark DeWolfe, Bishop

Paul Moore, and the caring congregants from All Souls in New York. We can hunker down in the trench and embrace those below the poverty line, the I.V. drug users, the gays, the prostitutes, the bisexuals, all of the youngsters (teenagers. children and babies), who are rapidly becoming the highest risk group for the dread disease.

AIDS and AFRAIDS move among us, threatening to create a new class of lepers. May we be granted the wisdom to hear and to comprehend Albert Camus' judgment that in the course of experiencing a plague, "there are more things to admire than there are things to despise about human beings."

*Frank Brown, Public Broadcast Radio, November 1, 1989.

# 4

# ...In The Company Of Persons With Disabilities

# Idiot Child

by Sidney Clouts

A solemn reverberating gold
sullened the sky and that is why
I took my tireless dolt
to run on the grass,
my dear dumb human colt
to thud on the green grass
looking up wild at the wildness he loved
of the tearing sky.

He leapt like a big stone
that starts at the brink
of a crude slope loosened by water.
Hardly could I bear to see
though I had watched him
a multitude, tiring never at all
to see him lock his clumsy hands
and fall on the ground with glee.
Good child, I said, though he will never hear me,
dearest child, when you were long ago born
unrespectably silent,
I did not hate you at all with such painful tenderness.
I was a long time preparing for my love.

What sealed you when you were born?
I stood in the dawn room
praying death into your cot where uninhabitant
you lay unborn.
Unborn?
O womanless child, pay wild
reverberant stones into the holes of snakes,
more perfect than your being and yet not made
even with such balked purposes:
torn edges of a dream that cannot sleep,
of sleep whose dreaming flares on a moonless mound.

*Go wriggle your lenient fingers in the grass*
*sparing the snails with terrible natural sense:*
*ballooned your jaw with subtle symmetry,*
*unfeebled grace, yet feeble beauty blown*
*into disreputable clownishness.*

*O severed race, blood nearest, sinless child,*
*watch me if you can watch me one slow*
*second as I stand upon the ground,*
*this actual spot of balance where I suffer*
*eyes that so painfully*
*love and respect your driven dance,*
*that living I must undesperately fall*
*the direst slope that any one can fall*
*the cruellest desperation that you fall*
*in stricken silence falling as you fall.*

# LESSONS FROM OUR DAUGHTER GRACIA (1977)

Sidney Clouts' poem, "Idiot Child," is an astonishingly accurate description of how a parent of a severely disabled child feels. When my wife, Cathe, and I met Sidney Clouts, we asked if, indeed, he was the parent of such a child. He replied that he was not. His experience had come from close observation of such a child born into the family of a close friend. The ability to evoke the experience of this special child-parent relationship is a rare gift, and his poem is a rare creation. It provides a setting for commentary about our daughter, Gracia, and lessons she teaches.

Gracia is not our only child. She has two siblings, Tyler and Melissa. All three of our children teach us lessons, just as all children teach us. However, I am presumptuous enough to say that lessons taught by Gracia are "special." Not only in the private sense that they are meant for us, her parents, but "special" in that they throw a rare kind of light on dim aspects of our commonly shared human experience.

Some of these lessons are personal and some involve the society in which we live. I comment on both types, after a word of introduction to Gracia herself.

Gracia is 13 years old chronologically, but operates at a mental age of between six months and two years. She has never spoken. There is no reason to rehearse the various medical labels which have been affixed to her over the years. Cathe recognized that something was wrong with her when she was less than six months old.

It suffices to say that she is utterly different from most people around her and from those with whom she comes in contact. It is her distance from the customary norms of socially acceptable behavior which occasions the first lesson.

This lesson concerns the world that we and Gracia inhabit. We all want a world that is orderly and predictable and will conform, at least in the main, to our standards and expectations. A world which blends into the pictures of proper conduct we carry around in our heads. Since Gracia does not conform, her often bizarre behavior and the public reactions which it attracts set up conflicts in her mother, her siblings, and in me. The inner conflicts occasionally spill over into anger directed at her and at those who stare at her in affronted astonishment. Another father of a severely disturbed child (and every parent of a disturbed child knows the feeling) lashes out angrily at the situation. He writes:

*"What people cannot stand to think is that a child such as you was born in the ordinary way and not dumped on our doorstep by some night traveling devil or mailed to the mother in installments (sender's name withheld) or bought cheap at Woolworth's. It's justice, really, gone sour right before your eyes. Folks can't bear to think that it happens to the innocent such as themselves so they dream up sins for your sponsors to have committed. In other words, they don't like a universe that's absurd; a universe they can't understand. They can't bear the evidence of a quite impersonal, inexplicable, organic mishap."*

I relate to that father's anger. I can identify with his thrashing about and his attempt to justify and somehow to equalize his pain. But even though I can relate to it, his anger gets in his own way; and he misses the really important lesson which his child (and my daughter) teaches, namely that the cosmos does not conform to our standards, as much as we might desire it. Gracia, and children like her, represent what amounts to a different universe. Once we accept this fact and are prepared to deal with it on its own terms, that universe is, by turns, incredibly beautiful and paralyzing frightening. In a very real sense, these "exceptional" children are our humanity — the intricate and profound cellular composition which constitutes us—emerged in a totally different "cellular dance."

*Twelve billion cells . . . and more*
*the unmapped untapped*
*internal infinity we orbit,*

*Chasing eternity determinedly,*
*we deface space*
*in so many spent races,*

*While our connate constellation*
*cries out piteously*
*imploring us for a piece of salvation,*

*Hounded and haunted by undiscovery,*
*our impotence, and inability,*
*we rush to escape the gravity.*

Once we find the courage to confront the astonishing fact of difference, something extraordinary happens. We discover that this profoundly different humanity has the power to draw from us aspects of our own humanity (some radiant, some hideous) which we would not have otherwise acknowledged. The more we are compelled to acknowledge the breadth and depth of the differences incorporated in our humanity, the more we can accept, then love the differences manifested in the humanity of other people.

In this connection I recall the work of the gifted photographer, Diane Arbus. Her photographs have been exhibited in the Museum of Modern Art and are published in a substantial volume. Her subjects are primarily social outcasts, rejects, misfits. The extraordinary thing about her pictures is not the subject matter, but the fact that the photographs avoid any kind of cloying sentimentality or artful attempts to produce pity in the viewers. Diane Arbus' photographs restate the second lesson which we have learned from Gracia: beware of pity! Beware of pity for yourself, for her, or pity for others. As an emotion, pity is counterproductive, serving only our spurious needs for self-gratification. Pity clogs and pollutes the channels of true feeling and deep compassion.

Hand in hand with pity goes the need to determine purpose. "Pity" asks the question, "Why did this have to happen?" and "Purpose" is always there ready to step forward with some facile or fatuous answer. This traditional relationship between pity and purpose is terribly difficult to escape. It runs through Judaism and Christianity. The tradition stretches from the mournful reasonings of those three "comforters" who showed up to tell Job why he was camped out on his dung heap to the mock oriental epigram of Sakini, in the play, *Teahouse of the August Moon*. According to Sakini, "Pain makes us think, thinking makes us wise, wisdom makes life endurable."

Baloney! It is our ability and our willingness to deal with reality on its own terms that makes reality meaningful, us wise, and life endurable. I am continually amazed by the prevalence of cut-rate Sakinis who always stand ready to offer "purposes" for Gracia (complete with silver linings). Cathe and I have been told that Gracia was "sent to us" in order that we might be better prepared to give comfort and solace to other people who were "afflicted" with similar children. Or that she was sent because we were strong enough to learn from her and provide for her without breaking. Or for reasons God chooses not to vouchsafe but, nonetheless, we'll discover one day.

Such attempts to discover some kind of purpose are inappropriate because they always start at the wrong end of the situation. They start with some pre-established ideal of "purpose," then attempt to fit reality to that purpose rather than start with the reality — regardless of how jagged, painful and appalling that reality may seem. A willingness to start with the reality is at the center of one of Cathe's poems.

# Sail Free Survivor

*I am a survivor.*
*You wince audibly*
   *as though it were*
*horrific*
   *to survive*
   *and keep myself*
*intact, alive*
*on my bleak moving raft*
*licking drying lips*
*and open sores*
*clasping close singed*
*dreams*
*recalling Icarus'*
*flight was*
   *doomed. He was no survivor.*
*You offer high*
*wires, but*
   *they are for skilled*
*practitioners*
*for whom soaring is a*
*well-rehearsed*
*affair. No.*
   *I uncork with caring*
*the precious balm*
   *of my dreams,*
*my connection to the universe,*
*sensualizing*
   *massaging the suggestive*
*oil into the erosions.*
*I sail free on my expansions.*

Gracia has her own standards of measurement, her own rhythms, her own periods of advance and retreat. These are her realities. These are the things we battle or deal with. We, and those working with her, wait for the signals that a "good time" is coming and then we do all that we can to teach her and train her while she is at a receptive "place," before her systems "close down" again. Cathe used the term "sail free" in her poem. "Sail free" has a special nautical meaning: to sail with the wind more than 6 points off dead ahead, letting out all your sails and boom. That is what we do during Gracia's "up" periods. She remains and probably always will remain "off course"—that is the reality with which we start. One deals with one's reality as honestly as one can in hope, but not necessarily expectation, that one can make the reality meaningful.

In Pennsylvania, the reality of Gracia's condition prompted us to seek a place for her in a residential environment. The Camphill Special School provided what we were seeking, namely a loving community where children with different disabilities and handicaps lived with families and "normal children." We learned that Gracia (operating as she does at the developmental level of a one-year-old) needs a *loving community* because it is only within the context of such a community that she feels secure enough to be fully present at any time.

It is within its loving community that each church and fellowship also has great opportunity to learn and to teach the same lessons which the exceptional child teaches its parents. No institution in our society is better equipped to learn and to teach acceptance and support to the disabled and their families. Acceptance and support means people who are willing to listen and learn about differences and disabilities without pity or advice-giving purposiveness. The act of simply making oneself available can be a profound act of healing ministry. As Daniel Berrigan has said (in a very different context): "Don't just do something; stand there!" The profound richness contained in the moments when we "stand there" is indicated in a short poem which Cathe wrote after a particularly good visit with Gracia at her school in Pennsylvania.

## Precious Time I

*The incredible*
*of being   together*
*whole*
*inside of now*
*on an*
*afternoon of*
*Autumn sunlight*
*streaking*
*s t r e t c h i n g*
*the soon to fade*
*colours*
*wafts   of   wildflowers*
*scents of potatoes*
*in season*
*amid*
*crushed rustles*
*leaves of*
*moments   gone   by*
*this is*
*a sweet profusion*
*of everything*
*beautiful*
*embracing you*

Being present to the "exceptional person" himself or herself can be a richly rewarding experience. Conversely, when such an opportunity is missed or forsaken, profoundly serious consequences can result. Let me offer an example. Years ago when I was on sabbatical and living temporarily in an affluent suburb, we occasionally attended area suburban churches, one of which boasted an enormous, well-equipped, splendidly staffed and dedicated church school. The school's director told us proudly that the school even provided instruction for "exceptional" children and led us to a room set well apart from the Religious Education wing. There, five children ranging in age from three to early teens were being watched over by a teacher. The children were all "exceptional," but the severity of their individual disabilities differed markedly. I do not know what lessons those exceptional children were learning in their isolated classroom, but I suggest that the rest of the church school was learning the lesson that exceptional children—regardless of the degree of severity of their condition—should be segregated from the "normals." It is an unfortunate lesson because children (like adults) learn to fear and reject what they are segregated from.

It is my conviction that churches should exemplify and teach that the children and the community develop in relationship to each other and that the "exceptional child," certainly no less and perhaps more than his/her normal counterpart, makes a *profound* contribution to the environing community's understanding of itself and of the surrounding world every day.

# First Times

*The day you discovered*
*the sky was*
*blue*
*I mean truly*
*BLUE*
*shot right through*
*with hue so strong*
*you seemed*
*uncertain*
*of its right*
*to belong*
*in*
*your universe*
*where skies*
*invade the day*
*with haze*
*clung to creaking cranes*
*a merciless maze*
*of grays*

*you ran pointing*
*anointing the air*
*with your ecstacy*

It is the kind of rediscovery of life's wonders, experienced in extraordinary new ways by our exceptional children, that leads us to a new awareness of how wonderful they really are. It took Gracia eight years to learn how to turn a doorknob. The day she discovered that by turning a doorknob, you can open a door and move through it into a whole new world was a day of extraordinary gaiety. The door, the knob, the world itself took on new meaning. We could not believe it. We put her in a room and closed the door and waited. Sure enough the doorknob turned, and out she came. We did it again, and again she would emerge, beaming and chuckling, to our mutual delight. Having exercised this hard earned skill of turning the doorknob, opened a new level of awareness for the three of us.

Massachusetts has a law—Bill 766—which guarantees the educational rights of exceptional children. The Federal Law 94-142 (1975) also safeguards those rights. Every child regardless of the kind or degree of disability now has the right to an education appropriate to his or her *needs*. But the law is no substitute for the supportive community our churches can provide. Support in terms of sustaining, caring, and sharing salves social injury. By giving of itself and being prepared to receive the often bizzare and always wonderful gifts these children can provide, the church is immensely enriched.

We have been working with Bill 766 on Gracia's behalf; but at present, Gracia receives only a portion of the care to which she is legally and morally entitled. Both she and we need that law. But the law—no matter how excellent and comprehensive—is no substitute for love and what love can accomplish.

# Homage III

*I had wandered aimlessly*
*through the drab*
*corridors of anonymity*
*unbeckoned*
*until your presence*
*mesmerized my soul*
*and I reckoned*
*myself as I*
*sensed you*
*wanting to share*
*in you and me*
*the gift to see and dare*
*to grope and grasp*
*blindly.*
*I am alive now*
*reborn*
*with your soaring energy*
*shorn*
*of death's tremors*
*I stand*
*in this sudden sun-shafted*
*lily-filled sanctuary*
*hoarded with the glorious*
*pronouncement of resurrection*
*from within your hand.*

# COULDN'T GOD HAVE
## MADE YOU BETTER?

*"People should only see how they look when they're looking at me."*
*"It's hard to dance in a wheelchair. Not impossible, just hard...and with the right person, wonderful."*
*"I have no interest in saying, 'Look at me,' I have a huge interest in saying, 'Don't look away.'"*[1]

Disabled people speak. Listen. Don't "look away." One out of every eight of us in the U.S. has a major disability, a serious condition that restricts that person's way of living in the world. One out of eight of us! They comprise a minority of between 35 and 37 million persons. A minority that one study has called "unexpected." Any minority that is unexpected is also oppressed.

I speak of persons who live with a developmental, a mental, a physical, or a sensory disability. I know two members of that population intimately; they are my daughters. One has a severe language/learning disability. Her condition is complicated by the fact that she also has a moderate to severe congental bi-lateral hearing disability. Her condition does not prevent her from functioning in the world. Our other daughter resides in a residential facility. She is a severely retarded, behaviorally disturbed adult who functions at a preschool developmental level.

Because I am the father of two disabled persons, I am empathetic to awkward and negative feelings which many families of the disabled harbor: shame, at having a disabled family member; fear of what others will think; rejection of sympathy which, even when delivered with best intentions, appears false or patronizing. I can identify with those feelings. I have experienced all of them. I am not substantially disabled. I know that people have a hard time knowing how to respond to people who are significantly disabled, and a harder time knowing how to be natural and present to people with such disabilities.

A chasm exists between people who are able-bodied and people who are disabled. Reasons for the chasm can be summed up in a single word: "Attitude". Attitude underlies our difficulty or inability to fully accept a person with a disabling condition. Our socially conditioned attitude works to discourage, if not to prevent, full acknowledgment and acceptance of those who are disabled. Words to describe persons with various disabilities come and go as disabled groups struggle for full acceptance and appreciation in our society.

Many people still use the word "handicapped" to identify people with disabilities. "Handicapped" is currently considered to be a pejorative term in most circles. Consider its history. It describes a begging, supplicating posture wherein the disabled person crouches, *cap-in-hand,* hoping to catch a coin that might be flipped from an able-bodied passer by.

A move to reinstate the term "handicapped" was recently raised in a regional newspaper of the deaf. The writer claimed that "handicapped" implied able but in need of assistance to equalize advantages, as in a golf handicap. He seemed unaware of the historical origins of the term. He felt "disabled" implied inability, but that handicap was predicated on ability. "Physically or mentally challenged" rather than either "handicapped" or "disabled" also have been proposed by physically disabled groups. The label war is a struggle against an historical tide of verbal slander and social stigma meted out to persons with disabilities.

Think of the words we have used for the mentally disabled. Dummy! Imbecile! Idiot! Retard! Fool! Moron! In our society the full use of one's mental capacity is considered essential to success in life. We place enormous store in mind over matter. Such negative naming encourages an attitude that identifies the mentally disabled as "weak links" in the human chain.

But when you consider that the disabled person functions in society as a result of having *overcome* obstacles that we are oblivious to, the weak link analogy breaks apart—overwhelmed by the courage, tenacity and strength of the disabled individuals and communities. They are physically or mentally challenged by their condition. And we are challenged to understand our attitudes and the value of disabled persons within our social structures.

Where does our negative attitude originate? Ancient cultures, such as Egyptian, Chinese, and Roman civilizations killed, or left to die babies with any deformity. Subsequent civilizations have been less sanguinary but equally disdainful of deformity and disability.

In the Hebrew Scriptures, Leviticus, Chapter 22, devoted to the Deuteronomic law, we read the instruction that those who have anything called a "blemish" are not permitted to present an offering to Yahweh. That tells us something about the position of persons with disabilities within the community of ancient Israel.

The image of God here is that of an all-powerful, all-encompassing monarch, perfect in every degree and regard, and desirous of perfection from those who would worship "Him." That particular scriptural admonition is one of the underpinnings of the argument against permitting women to become priests in the Roman Catholic Church.

This is not the only understanding of the place of a person with disabilities in the Hebrew Scriptures. The prophet Jeremiah provides the image of God as a potter, who makes and endlessly remakes vessels until they are appropriate to God's use. The image is God as Creator who is able to restore whatever it is that needs mending. It is a step up from the perfection demanded by the monarch of Leviticus, but a condescension lingers. Nonetheless, Hebrew Scriptures do affirm inclusion of disabled persons among the chosen people and therefore deserving of human compassion.

In the Christian Scriptures, the situation is worse. The God as personified in the figure of Jesus of Nazareth invited the overtly disabled to come to him. The disabled came to Jesus to be cured because he spoke openly to them and identified with their suffering, with their *dis-ease*. They experienced healing in his presence, a healing which goes beyond concepts of cure or therapy but which has been interpreted literally and negatively throughout Christendom. True healing reflects an acceptance that envelops the whole person, disability and all. At its best, the Church has sought to embody and to emulate this accepting, empowering attitude toward the disabled. At its worst, it has condemned disfigurement and disability as God's judgement, evidence of the Devil, a condition to be cured or condemned.

Unfortunately, the Church has very rarely been at its best in this matter. More often, the Church has lurched in the direction of Martin Luther's attitude toward the disabled. Luther was of the opinion that the mentally retarded (he called them "changelings") had no souls; that they were simply "masses of flesh." For Luther, it was in the devil's power to corrupt people who have reason and souls. He went on to say that the devil sits in the changeling in the place where the soul should have been. "They should be taken and drowned!" So spoke the leader of the Reformation.

Before we rush to judgment we should remember that Luther was a product of his time, just as we are products of ours. Before we dismiss Luther's grotesquerie out of hand, we might look at the social norms that separate *us* and isolate *us* from the disabled and see if there is any devil that dwells among us.

Consider how our society works to make those of us who are able-bodied in mind and spirit feel self-conscious about what we eat and drink and wear and do. The physicist Freeman Dyson, recalled the occasion when his 5-year-old stepdaughter came in and saw him standing naked in his bedroom. She stared at his skinny frame and said, "Did God make you like that?"When he said, "Yes," she said, "Couldn't God have made you better?"

95

That is a message that media hammer home relentlessly: Couldn't God have made you better? To be content, to accept what you are is not to be normal. A person who admits to normality does so only under extreme provocation. When overburdened by demands, you throw up your hands in depair and say, "Well, after all, I'm only human!"

If the abled are feeling insecure about themselves, the presence of a developmentally or mentally disabled person heightens their feelings of insecurity and fear. We able-bodied individuals are often willing to do *with* and for the disabled but extremely hesitant to receive *from* the disabled. To receive *from* the disabled keys directly into our insecurity.

A profound fear is evoked in us when we encounter a disabled person. The fear relates to suffering. Our awareness of the fragility of our human condition is heightened by the sight of disabled persons. I have seen this fear. I have seen it in the eyes of strangers as I walk with my daughter through streets and shops.

The fear is based on belief that my daughter is suffering. People project their own fears of suffering, of loneliness, of weakness, of insecurity on her. And they fear that her suffering is contagious.

The best way to address such fear is to address the pretensions which condition the way we live. The first pretension, enshrined in the pedagogy of pop psychology, is spelled out in a very simple phrase: "I'm OK, You're OK." I am grateful to William Sloane Coffin, Jr., former minister of Riverside Church and current director of SANE/Freeze, who gives lie to this kind of psycho-babble. The truth, said Bill, is: "I'm *not* OK. And *you're* not OK. And *that's* OK."

To be limited, to be partial, to be incomplete, is to partake of the human condition. It is to be part and parcel of creation and we ought to be able to rejoice in it! Emerson summed it up when he observed that "Everything God made has a crack in it!"

From the most gifted to the neediest, all of us are woven into the fabric of existence—imperfections, warts and all.

To deny that truth is to turn one's back on everything that makes a civilized world civilized. We who think of ourselves as non-disabled begin to realize that we too live with limitations. Be it the glasses that I wear to see ably or the hearing aid that I wear if I am to hear spoken words or music. Certainly these are not severe disabilities but the ultimate difference is in degree, not in kind.

No less than the disabled we must depend upon each other, if life is going to be livable. And there is a transformative change when we, as a religious community, take active steps to welcome the disabled into our midst. This change can be sweeping, to the point of challenging and changing our concept of God.

One of the penetrating criticisms leveled by feminist theologians has been that in a male-dominated society God is male. Black theologians pointed out that in a white-dominated society God is white. For the heterosexual, homophobic congregation God is oriented to a heterosexual society. Doesn't the same judgment apply to an able-bodied society?

Liberation theologians say that God must be a God of the oppressed, the lonely, the suffering, the poor—and yes, the disabled. God is the healing that fills the limitations in all our beings, bodied able and bodied disabled alike. It is by being honest and forthright about our limitations that we become accessible to a power that can restore us. The person who is disabled can be the instrument of the non-disabled person's liberation from the myth that we are self-reliant and from the burden of attempting to reconcile that myth with the facts of life.

In return, able-bodied persons can be freed from the fear we experience. The church community that seriously works to integrate mentally and physically disabled persons provides itself with an extraordinary opportunity for spiritual growth and nourishment. The tragedy is that it is usually a missed opportunity in one church after another. It has not been uncommon for our congregations to disregard sensory and physical accessibility. It has not been uncommon to refuse to educate significantly disabled children in our educational programs. And when we have done so, we have resorted to separate and unequal responses to such children.

An alternative script for physically and mentally challenged members and friends comes from the annals of the First Unitarian Church in San Francisco. A warm welcome was extended and cooperative accommodation made for a youth with substantial mental retardation in one of the Sunday classes in 1988. His class took a field trip to view elephant seals at a nearby reserve in the spring of 1989. Following the trip, his teacher wrote a letter to the director of religious education which read as follows:

*"Our outing was fun and informative. We made a special effort to involve all of the children, and Nathan was able to join us. Although he has overtly little in common with the others, it was really heart-warming and exciting to witness the acceptance of the others toward him, the ease and the comfort he felt with them, and the sharing of talent and knowledge, and understanding, among everyone.*

*We walked on a tour with the ranger, who talked to us about the elephant seals. The ranger pointed out one female seal who had gotten wedged between two large sand dunes. There was no way of determining at that time if she would be able to make it back to the water. Nathan asked if he could carry her back. The ranger stated that they couldn't do anything which would interfere with Nature.*

*Now, that answer seemed good enough for all of us in the group, but Nathan's facial expression carried an empathy that transcended words. As all of us moved on down to the next viewing area, Nathan dropped my hand and started toward the water. Instinctively, he seemed to know that water was the lifeblood of this animal, and was going to carry some over to the seal, much like that of a parent, putting an extra blanket on a child at night—an act of unconditional love.*

*We diverted his attention and moved on, but each of us in our own way realized that, although we may look and act differently from each other, we are all of the same family.*

*One of the class members summed it up perfectly: 'I guess getting all A's doesn't mean you're smart.'"[2]*

[1]from *Ordinary Moments,* Alan Brightman, Ed., University Park Press, Baltimore, 1984.

[2]Used with permission of the author, Nathan and Nathan's parent.

# GRACIA II (1986)

*Since "Gracia I," several years have passed. Gracia, Cathe and I have changed. Cathe more than I, since, in the interim, she has completed graduate studies and moved from being a teaching assistant to a professional in Special Education. Gracia has changed in the sense that she has aged into adulthood, and her problems have grown in complexity.*

*Gracia continues to function at profoundly to severely retarded levels. "Severely retarded" connotes an IQ level between 20 and 35. In terms of age ability, Gracia functions between the capabilities of a twelve-month infant and thirty-six month child. Her problems are compounded by her tendency to self-injurious behavior. In the adolescent interim Gracia's self-injurious behavior increased to a point of threatening permanent and profound self-injury. This fact led us to adopt one of the most sweeping and irreversible responses to her condition, the use of drugs, to control self-injurious behavior, which had not diminished with years of intensive behavior modification programs. Every day Gracia swallowed 1200 milligrams of Thorazine. If you or I were to take 50 milligrams of Thorazine we would become sleepy and unable to function adequately. For some reason which medical science does not understand, this drug is metabolized differently in most severely retarded, self-injurious individuals. It often requires massive dosages by any standard to get pacifying results.*

*For Gracia the result is that she seldom strikes herself. That is the "good news." The "bad news" is that it resulted in a limping, uneven gait and right arm posturing—exacerbating a congenital weakness in the right side of her body and making it difficult for her to walk, run, or enjoy an agile body.*

*Although Gracia is a much-loved severely retarded person, she is also a member of a particular class, an unloved underclass within our society. Our previous statement described Gracia, the individual, our daughter. These remarks focus on Gracia as a member of a social class. Our comments therefore relate to the needs of that class, as reflected in Gracia's and our own experience.*

According to the 1985 President's Commission on Mental Retardation, there are 6,900,000 retarded people in the United States; 6,200,000 of them are classified as mildly and moderately retarded.*These are persons who, by and large, are not readily identifiable as different from the rest of the population. They are like fish in the human sea. Some swim slower or more awkwardly, but they still swim. Which leaves 700,000 people who are severely or profoundly retarded. They do *not* swim like the rest of us in the human sea. Many of them do not paddle or even float. Without constant attention they would sink like stones. Gracia is one of those. Reflecting on this fact occasions the first of the current lessons Gracia teaches: a lesson in the matter of assigning value and worth to human beings.

Each one of us has known (in our heart of hearts) that we are worth something. Each one of us appreciates (at some level) that we are needed and wanted and valued—by many or by a few. In spite of what we may be tempted to say to the contrary (the rhetoric about how the world will go on without us), we who are ordinary people live and act and believe that we are necessary. But what about the not-so-ordinary people? What about the people who "produce" nothing? My response to such a query is that people are people, regardless of what they do (or don't do), by virtue of our common humanity.

*President's Committee on Mental Retardation, Miles Santamour Commission. *The Boston Globe,* "Parade Magazine," 8/25/85.

If someone is valuable as a human being, then anyone is valuable as a human being. And yet the one fundamental piece of *evidence* testifying to the fact that some people are value-able and some people are value-less is the presence in our society of "institutions," and the concept of "institution-alization." Gracia resides in an "institution." It is perhaps the best "institutional program" that her state and most states have to offer a person functioning at Gracia's level. The state pays people to train and take care of her; it provides her with food, shelter, medicine; it is kind to her. For all of these things we are grateful. What we are not grateful for is the whole concept of "institutional" that continually threatens or controls Gracia and what that means for her and for this society.

To be institutionalized means to be denied one's personhood. It means to be denied liberty and freedom of movement without having committed a crime. It means to be denied the opportunity to live in an ordinary community. It means to be denied the right to eat when you want and what you want. It means to be denied the right to sleep where you want and with whom you want. It means to be denied the right to travel. It means to be denied the right to meaningful, rewarding work. It means to be denied the rites of passage into society at every level. To be institutionalized means to acknowledge that keepers have more value than the kept. But by some curious logic, the institutional keepers are *themselves* devalued by the members of the environing society, who view people-keeping institutions with deeply contradictory emotions.

Educator, author and advocate Burt Blatt has written: "There is a lesson to be learned from history. The lesson is that it is impossible to decently segregate large numbers of devalued people who are cared for by devalued attendants. And all of these people are separated from a society that does not know or care what happens to them, and will learn not to care about them. Chronic segregation—wherever it is found—invariably leads to degradation, dehumanization, pain, torment."*

The evidence to support Mr. Blatt's assertion is everywhere apparent. Chronic segregation—from the isolation cells of a maximum security prison to the most humane and caring nursing facility for the elderly—leads to degradation, dehumanization, pain, and torment. These conditions may be excruciatingly apparent (as revealed in the course of a governmental investigation into correctional facility abuses) or they may be velvet gloved, subtle, and easily ignored (as in the case of some of the well-equipped, smoothly operated nursing facilities). But the conditions of institutionalism are there.

## Lessening of the Parts

*We spent you this morning.*
*"Professionals" we call ourselves.*
*We scattered you, rearranged*
*in painless minutiae,*
*Never to gather you in again.*

*We dissected you this morning.*
*So precise were we*
*In our subsecting, terrified*
*of reviving you,*
*We fixed on micro-tissue.*

*We voided you this morning.*
*Eighteen of us stood tall,*
*We shook hands, self-satisfied,*
*by all the dried pages,*
*Lessening your outrageous life.*

*In and Out of Books,* review of "The Family Papers: A Return to Purgatory," Blatt, Burton, p. 175.

What is the answer to this situation? "Replace the big, anonymous institutions with small group homes. Permit residents to move freely in the community." It is a praiseworthy sentiment; a call for us to marshall our efforts toward converting this inhospitable society into a more caring environment for all people.

And the creation of such an environment certainly strikes us as noble and necessary. However, the precipitous closing of institutions (prompted less from humanitarian motives than from state and federal budgetary deficits) has cast thousands not into a more humane and caring society, but into a society that disdains and disregards them at best— exploits and destroys them at worst.

"Small is beautiful" has become an automatism in deinstitutionalization circles. We have overgeneralized small and large to suit social convenience and to assuage our fears. In fact, institutionalization and its counterpart, abuse, occurs in biological homes, foster placements, small community facilities, medium housing units, and large anonymous structures. It occurs in remote state hospitals or supervised downtown apartments. It occurs in day rehabilitation units, sheltered workshops or community workplaces.

Institutionalism is not a place. It is a process. It is a particular pattern of relating: a pattern which retains dependency and discourages enablement. Institutionalism encourages only those abilities which suit the convenience of the caregivers (family members, professionals, community providers).

"The environments people need are more often obtainable and more easily created in the heterogeneous normal world," Burton Blatt commented. But it was the uniqueness of each personal need, not the codification of general circumstances, that he actually emphasized in defining the perspective of successful survival in the human sea.

Indeed, regardless of size or location, the establishment of personal, dependable and humanitarian conditions which relate to the environing heterogeneous community is a way out of this morass. Humane, heterogeneous, enabling atmospheres throughout every phrase of deinstitutionalism and within each facility are critical.

Gracia's adult life has indicated that it is possible for well-designed, medium-sized facilities to provide the socially stimulating, caring, rewarding and safe environments that a person like Gracia needs. But her experiences also have shown that we must all continually monitor and critique every facility: large, medium, small (including natural and foster homes) to prevent the victimizing institutionalizing of persons with severe, profound or any disabilities.

We are all of a piece. From generation to generation. From person to person. From need to need. In attempting to meet Gracia's adult needs over the past few years we have come to appreciate the universality of her condition and the rudiments of a social prescription.

After years requiring constant supervision, Gracia gained greater freedom. She became well enough to move independently from place to place, at will. In fact she experienced more freedom than would be available in many small community homes, because of the availablity of ample staff and a protective, surrounding environment in a receptive community.

Gracia developed a rewarding vocation through her educational program. She learned to be one of two lunch-time janitors. She eagerly rolled out the trash barrel, stacked chairs, and cleared tables. When she was born we never considered trash collection as a proud vocation. Social attitudes had stunted such vision! Our daughter's vocation as janitor has given us great pleasure and pride. To know and name a vocation that brings pleasure and contributes to community need is a powerful element.

Gracia also experienced a meaningful personal relationship with a peer. As the social worker put it protectively, "Another client has taken a liking to Gracia." Cause for great celebration! Gracia experienced having a man care significantly for her. Someone who saw her come into a room and actually moved across that room to be near her. Someone who stroked her arm and occasionally held her loosely at the waist. Someone whose touch Gracia accepted (and may have even welcomed!).

To value one person IS to value all persons. To value those who cannot "produce" is to value those who can. And so we seek answers with more urgency as larger facilities close and the economy worsens. As the problems of have and have not accrue. Pursuit of answers lies within as well as beyond the confines of existing facilities. It lies in touching the universality of our souls and responding through the loving communities around us:

## Thinking of Lovers

*In the setting sun,*
*Rays sprayed across cirrus clouds,*
*I move into terror and joy,*
*Overcome.*
*An absurd ache - loving (!)*
*The boundlessly beautiful:*
*A milkweed pod's breath of birds*
*bursting across an infestation*
*Of an old woman's joyful smile*
*At the sight of her son's face,*
*Messages to be confessed*
*In a young daughter's glance,*
*Fingers entwined in voicelessness;*
*Thinking of lovers.*
*As you touch your mother's hands,*
*I hum an old nursery song*
*From the book of a million years.*

# 5

## ...In The Struggle For For Racial Justice

# THE LONG CONFUSION
## ABOUT BLACK EMPOWERMENT

Hear again the profound prophecy of W.E.B. DuBois. "The problem of the 20th century is the problem of the color line—the relation of the darker to the lighter races in Asia, Africa, America, and the islands of the sea."[1] He wrote these words in 1903. The fact that we have yet to grasp their significance accounts in large measure for our "long confusion" about black empowerment.

In the century of Freud and Marx and Einstein, of two world wars and the threat of nuclear annihilation of the planet, it is easy to dismiss DuBois' statement as hyperbole. That would be a mistake. Consider the fact that the issue of race lies at the heart of so many of the issues confronting us in our common life. So many of the profound antagonisms of our time manifest a racial component at their core. From the entrance of students of color into the educational process to the problem of oil and its distribution, from the suppression of minorities to the exploitation of the world's peoples, the issue of race seems to be always with us.

Why should "the color line" be a problem for this particular century? Because, in the words of black theologian Cornell West, "The notion that black people are human beings is a relatively new discovery in the modern West."[2] In previous centuries the color line was not a problem because race was not an issue. But, as Octavio Paz reminds us, this century has been a century when all of the peoples of color, who have lived for so long in a kind of twilight zone of semi-consciousness in the Western world, have begun to assert themselves. According to Paz, "One day in the 20th century, the subterranean world blew up. This explosion hasn't yet ended and its splendor has illumined the agony of the age."[3] The focus of the agony is the color line.

During the 1950s when I was in theological school reading Paul Tillich and Karl Barth and Reinhold Niebuhr, no one ever told me that I was reading "white theology." It wasn't until the late 1960s that theologians began to point out that the theology I was reading—Catholic, Protestant, conservative, and liberal—was implicitly white and male.

It was not until the late 1960s, with the work of Professor James Cone and Pastor Albert Cleage, that the world of theology was confronted by the meaning of oppression and exploitation and the fact of oppressed and exploited people as being the central focus of theology. This shift occurred within the historical context of the Civil Rights movement. Its aim was to articulate the meanings of the phrase "black empowerment."

Black theology, rooted in the black American experience, provides linkages with the Third World* and with liberation initiatives throughout the world. It has had the effect of bonding African American blacks with other people of color who have experienced oppression, suffering, and exploitation at the hands of whites. Not least among these peoples are the Native Americans.

While the Civil Rights movement of the 1960s provided the context for the development of black theology, it also provided occasional articulation of the concerns of the native Americans in the context of oppression theology. In his book, *Custer Died For Your Sins,* Vine Deloria puts his finger on a singular problem by calling attention to the fact that people are always interested in the Native Americans' "plight."

> *"Indians have a plight. Other groups have difficulties, predicaments, quandaries, problems, troubles. Traditionally, we Indians have a plight. Our foremost plight is our transparency. People can just tell by looking at us what we want, what should be done to help us, how we feel, and what a real Indian is really like."[4]*

*A term which has rightly fallen into critical disrepute because of associated derogatory implications.

The condition of transparency is even more applicable to the African American than it is to the Native American. Ralph Ellison made explicit the case of black transparency in his novel, *Invisible Man;* James Baldwin alluded to it in his essays, *Nobody Knows My Name.* Black Empowerment became a way of saying, "You will not look through us any more. We demand that your attention be fixed upon the reality of our being and our need." Or, in the words of Ric Masten, "Look at me, fix me in your eye. I am here."[5]

Within the context of our denomination, the work of the Rev. Mark Morrison-Reed *(Black Pioneers in a White Denomination)* provides explicit testimony of the cruel truth that "transparency" can kill. Morrison-Reed tells the heartbreaking story of Egbert Ethelred Brown and his heroic struggle to establish Unitarian churches in Jamaica and Harlem, New York. At every turn this black pioneer experienced the crushing racism ingrained in a denomination that prided itself for its espousal of freedom and religious liberation. Morrison-Reed's book testifies that persons of color are not the only ones in need of liberation. White people need to be liberated, too; liberated from spurious ideas of power. We who are white need to be shown how our power "over" others has corrupted us and prevented us from achieving anything resembling a human community. It is our collective failure to fully understand this truth that has contributed to our long confusion. It has prevented us, even now, from being able to recognize our own oppression.

James Cone has written, "Racism is so embedded in the heart of American society that few, if any, whites can free themselves from it."[6] I interpret that to mean that what we are as white human beings has been shaped and molded by the forces of racism that course through our society at every level. I interpret *that* to mean that every person with a white skin has profited from racism in America. And I interpret *that* to mean that each one of us who is white has, at the very least, inherited social benefits which have been procured at the expense of black people's lives and well-being.

I have no interest in establishing my own or any other white person's guilt for this unjust situation. I have deep interest in taking steps to address and rectify it. The first step is a willingness to declare that, regardless of any benefits derived, the primacy of white power is morally wrong and the benefits are undeserved. One small but pivotal step. Because not to challenge this imbalance of power is to accept it as being morally correct and such acceptance, on your part or mine, defines us as "oppressors." "Oppressors!" I should add, who are themselves oppressed.

I contend that to live in a situation that is morally wrong and to derive benefits from that situation is to experience the weight of oppression at some psychic level. Can a people be benefitted and oppressed at the same time? Yes! We have the vivid example of the "Goodgermans" who did not awaken to their oppressive situation until it was too late. They were encouraged to cooperate and benefitted from Hitler's Reich even as their humanity was being filched away from them. To be "oppressed" is to be "defined, located, and set aside according to another's (in that case, Hitler's) perspective."[7] This is precisely what the word oppression means.

During the thirteen year history of the Third Reich, the Goodgermans acquiesced to genocide. Today, they and their children bear the weight of the Holocaust. Who can eradicate the weight that centuries of white supremacy have cast upon us as a people?

A white author and scholar, Robert Terry, drives to the heart of the issue. "To attack racism is to attack normalcy."[8] "American normalcy" refers to the social totality of which every one of us is a part, the totality in which we exist and apart from which we would not know who we are. For white people, "American normalcy" is so close, so obvious, so acceptable, that the task of gaining some perspective in order to examine and analyze it is almost impossible. Something like the fish attempting to get a perspective and analyze the water in which it swims and on which it depends for its very life.

112

And yet, in our deepest, clearest, most honest moments we know that white humanity is linked with a racist American normalcy. If American normalcy needs to be exposed, our "normal" way of doing things and living our lives needs to be confronted. This can be, and usually is, an unsettling experience, a painful experience.

The Black Empowerment Controversy within Unitarian Universalism was a painful confrontation with our own denominational brand of "normalcy" in race relations. The Black Unitarian Universalist Caucus which provoked the Controversy was, in the words of The Rev. Homer Jack, "impossible, irritating, and outrageous." "But then," continued Jack, "so is the birth of any idea of consequence. Revolution is never reasonable or rational."[9]

White Unitarian Universalists (like whites generally in American society) needed to be liberated from racist structures and from their own alienated humanity which is produced by those structures. Yet the means to such white liberation (a revolutionary idea) appeared "impossible, irritating and outrageous." To accomplish such a feat, black Unitarian Universalists first had to break into the consciousness of whites; second, had to provoke whites to a consciousness of the fact that racism is a white problem; and third, had to help whites ask not "what can we do to help you black folk?" but "what can we do to liberate ourselves from our racism?"The Black Empowerment Controversy can be understood as an instrumentality whose aim was to accomplish these three ends.

The Black Empowerment Controversy provided white members of this denomination with the opportunity to take upon themselves what James Cone has called "*the blackness of existence in the world*".[10] It provided those of us who are white with the occasion (albeit fragmented and distorted) to experience the human condition from a totally different perspective—the perspective of the poor, the captive, the oppressed. Namely, the perspective of those to whom the Judeo-Christian Scriptures were originally addressed and through whose lives they were intended to be interpreted.

White people cannot become black in any physical sense. Nor can white people (given our inheritances and our roles in the American status quo) easily become economically, socially, and politically exploited, humiliated, or abused. The human condition as defined by a skin pigmentation of color is simply not available to middle-class whites. But that does not mean that some consciousness of the meaning of blackness is totally beyond our grasp. There are avenues by which it can be encountered and embraced—at least metaphorically. "Blackness" describes the condition of the person who places him/herself in conflict with a demonic culture and suffers accordingly at the hands of that culture.[11]

Examples abound of white persons whose personal encounters with and conflict with the forces of oppression and inhumanity provided them with the experience of blackness and became avenues leading to their own liberation from demonic white power. I think immediately of Pastor Martin Niemoller. Niemoller spent from 1937 to 1945 in Nazi concentration camps. The experiences leading to his imprisonment and undergone during it provide a vivid example of "blackness." Poet Theodore Roethke has observed, "In a dark time, the eyes begin to see."

Similar possibilities exist for a church community that is willing to engage in the struggle against the principalities and the powers. One thinks of the Catholic Worker Movement and Dorothy Day; of St. Rose's Hospice and its volunteer orderly, Father Daniel Berrigan; one thinks of the various communities gathered in protest against the flagrant abuse of white power reflected in the military budget of this country. These are examples of communities taking upon themselves voluntarily the hard conditions with which persons of color must struggle *involuntarily*. By so doing, persons and communities gain purchase on the condition of blackness; by so doing, white, in effect, becomes black.

During the period know as the Black Empowerment Controversy, the Unitarian Universalist denomination was engaged in precisely this kind of struggle. The struggle was not unique to the denomination or, indeed, to our particular period in history. It is a struggle which occurs again and again because its significance transcends the empowerment of any particular group of persons at a particular moment in history. At the heart of the struggle is the authenticity of the religious enterprise. Nothing else. Nothing less.

The best way to understand the controversy is as a demand that Unitarian Universalists embrace a model of the church as being the instrument of oppressed communities throughout history. In other words, after oppression—blackness—is experienced, then one can understand and recognize God's liberating activity in history.

The liberal church is an historic structure. It has both the legal status and the moral authority to stand as a witness for moral goodness. Because of what we have been and what we are, we are empowered to become a center for gathering liberating change in our society.

Now is the time to move beyond the long confusion about Black Empowerment to a new and deeper understanding of what empowerment means for all peoples. We need not resurrect the Controversy, but we should recognize that the Controversy is a call for our resurrection. We need not return to the past, but we should discern the past's pattern in the present and do something to prevent its infecting and distorting the future.

What can we do? We can listen more carefully to the voices coming to us from the edge of our society. We can adopt modes of service (as opposed to modes of direction) which empower all who suffer from overt or covert oppression. We can expose and oppose the sources creating and maintaining the continuing human misery. And we can be guided by the words of an African-American poet, Amiri Baraka, that call for a new, transforming beginning:

> "We wade in the water
> America
> America
> We wade in the bleeding

*We wade in the screaming*
*in the unemployment*
*in the frustrated wives*
*and impotent husbands*
*of the dying middle*
*class,*
*in the anger of its*
*workers*
*its niggers*
*its wild intelligent*
*spics*
*its*
*brutalized*
*chicanos*
*its women out of work, again*
*Hymn poem for the passing into*
*for the change into*
*the transformation."*[12]

## NOTES

1. W. E. B. DuBois, "Of the Dawn of Freedom," Collected Essays, International Publishers, Atlanta, 1903.

2. Cornel West, *Prophecy Deliverance.* Westminster Press, Philadelphia, 1982.

3. Octavio Paz, "The New Analogy," 3rd Herbert Read Lecture, p. 25.

4. Vine Deloria, *Custer Died For Your Sins.* Delta Books, New York, 1978, p. 1

5. Ric Masten, Songbook.

6. James Cone, *Liberation: A Black Theology of Liberation.* Seabury Press, New York, 1972, p. 23.

7. ibid, p. 15. (parenthesis mine)

8. Robert W. Terry, "Active New Whiteness: Lighting a Damp Log." Paper delivered at Conference of American Society of Christian Ethics, Dayton, Ohio, 1972, p. 3.

9. Empowerment: The Report of the UUA Commission of Appraisal, June 1983, p. 25.

10. Cone, op. cit., p. 12.

11. Victor Carpenter, Minns Lectures, Pub. 1983, p. 66.

12. Amiri Baraka, "Reprise of One of A. G.'s Best Poems," Poetry of Amiri Baraka/LeRoi Jones. William Morrow & Co., 1979 (quoted in *Prophecy Deliverance,* op cit.).

# A KING AND A DUKE:
## When Images Conflict

I was ordained a Unitarian minister at Christ Church, a small Unitarian church located in Dorchester, one of the most heavily Roman Catholic sections of Boston. Christ Church, Dorchester had a history of struggle to keep its doors open. It survived largely through the help of the Benevolent Fraternity of Unitarian Universalist churches. I was its student minister, carrying on a ministry while attending the Harvard Divinity School. My ministry in Dorchester lasted less than two years. Shortly after I was ordained I moved to another church. Christ Church continued for a few years with other student ministers but finally surrendered to demographic shifts and was sold to an Hispanic Evangelical congregation.

Years passed. Then, on a winter night two decades after I had been ordained there, I decided, quite on the spur of the moment, to turn off the Boston Southeast expressway and make my way back to Dorchester. I wanted to see if the old building was still standing and what it looked like. After getting lost on the Dorchester streets, I finally found Dix street. The church was still there. The signs over the doors were in Spanish, proclaiming the hours of worship services and church school. I couldn't read the Spanish, but I could read another sign on the door. Someone had taken a can of white spray paint and written "KKK" across the door in large letters.

Six months later I drove by Christ Church again; the KKK insignia was gone, but the congregation had erected a chain-link fence six feet tall running the length of the church property and topped with strands of barbed wire. I suppose that the Hispanic congregation had been driven to adopt such a measure for its own protection. Score some kind of victory for the Klu Klux Klan.

Boston newspapers published two stories about the Klan's reappearance in the Boston area in the mid-1980s. The thrust of both stories had been to minimize the Klan's presence and its significance. Both of the major daily papers tended to dismiss the Klan's presence, and its power claim, as trivial, or ridiculous or both, an attitude that helped soothe and confirm Bostonian belief that THAT kind of racist "acting out" might be appropriate to some back-woods, hillbilly rednecks, but should not be taken seriously in liberal, enlightened Boston.

These feelings of local superiority were confirmed during a conversation I had with the reporter who wrote the story minimizing the Klan's power and activity. He referred to an earlier story he had written, calling attention to the Klan's presence in Boston, and told how he had been besieged by angry readers who refused to believe that such a pheno-menon as the Klan could possibly exist at all in the city which poet Whittier had once called "Christian liberty's chosen home, where none shall his neighbor's rights gainsay..." The facts say otherwise.

The facts of Klan activity in the city and the suburbs of Boston, in its schools, its work places, and in the prisons, all point to the manifestation of the KKK in Boston. To pro-claim ignorance of that presence or of its significance is an exercise in naivete and social myopia.

In the 1960s Rap Brown shocked this country by speaking a truth: "Violence is as American as apple pie." So is the Klan! It is as American as our continued reliance on violence and the threat of violence as means of resolving our social problems.

The Klan has been around for over a century. Its peak national strength occurred not during the Reconstruction Period, when it originated, but during the late 1920s, when it boasted nearly six million members. At that time the Klan could boast that one out of every eight white gentile

American males belonged to it. Former President Harry Truman was once a Klansman; so was Supreme Court Justice Hugo Black. During that period membership in the Klan was virtually a prerequisite for any Southern sheriff or deputy or, indeed, any other "law enforcement" officer. The Klan built an Imperial Palace in Atlanta, sent a "special ambassador" to Washington and considered buying Valparaiso University. Klan leader David Stevenson entertained serious aspirations toward the office of President of the United States. These aspirations suffered a serious setback due to his conviction for murder in 1928.

During the Depression the Klan's membership fell off significantly, but its practices, which included the use of violence and the threat of violence, continued to define the contours of race relations during the 1930s, the 1940s, and the 1950s.

Boston's current minimalizing of the indifference to the Klan's presence in the city represents a marked change in attitude. In 1922 ("heyday" of the Klan) when, in addition to being anti-Negro and anti-Jew, it was vociferously anti-Roman Catholic the then mayor of Boston, James Michael Curley, acted to ban all meetings of the Klan anywhere in the city whether on public or on private property. I am certain that if there is some anthropomorphic celestial backroom where Boston Irish Roman Catholic pols are gathered, "Honest Jim" Curley must be smiling through the cigar smoke to hear this WASP son of a Boston Republican father applaud his courageous and enlightened action.

Now the Klan welcomes Roman Catholics. Indeed, the Klan proselytizes in heavily Catholic areas (which also happen to be white working class areas) of this nation's cities. The Klan has shown a remarkable ability to exploit and manipulate the anger, frustration and confusion of ordinary working class white people in the North, East and West, as well as in the South. Where white workers are threatened with unemployment and inflation the Klan is there to fuel their fears with racist cries of "reverse discrimination" and "blame the niggers." Where whites were confused about busing in Boston, about school textbooks in West Virginia, about the rights of Chicanos and foreign-born workers along the US-Mexican border, about the possibility of multi-racial prison unity as tried at Napanoch Prison in New York—there the Klan is present, manipulating, exploiting and sowing racial hatred and social discord.

In 1975 David Duke, then National Director and Grand Wizard of the Klan in Louisiana, ran for the U.S. Senate from that state. He did not win, but he polled 11,000 votes. Duke made no secret of his Klan affiliation. In fact, he listed his position in the Klan as one of his qualifications for U.S. Senator—proof of his ability to represent and act as an advocate for the needs of white people. In the course of his campaign Duke made a statement in which he described the new appeal of the KKK.

> *"The Klan has all the effects of a mass movement. It's got the banners, the badges, the history, the heroes, the martyrs. It's got all the right things that can bring out the sort of dedication and religious fervor that any sort of movement needs to be ultimately successful. Second, the image of the Klan as a radical - in fact, an image which was not really inaccurate - a very strong anti-nigger image, anti-Jewish image in the country may not be a political disadvantage - that image may be an advantage. If America is headed toward more radical times, if its people really feel threatened, they're not going to want some kind of half measure. They're going to want something strong."*

In his own crazy, distorted way, Duke has hold of a truth. People *do* need "images," compelling images. Images of racist power and white supremacy, demonic though they be, *do* exercise a profound influence upon the imaginations and the lives of the fearful and threatened whites, whom he is addressing.

Images are important; images can organize one's life so that one can derive meaning and extension beyond one's self. Images serve to multiply reflected light. *Images are the very substance of religions!* David Duke and the KKK traffic in images, recognizing that these images exercise power in the imaginations of their followers.

But there is another man who knew the value and power of images on the imaginations and lives of others. The images which this man promoted and used to illuminate the life around him were of a wholly different magnitude and worth. His images were of an ennobled human condition, inspired, lifted up, blessed with divine nobility. On a sodden and muggy April night in a depressed part of Memphis, Tennessee, Martin Luther King, Jr. spoke to a discouraged band of garbage collectors.

> *"We got some difficult days ahead, but it really doesn't matter with me now. Because I've been to the mountaintop, I won't mind. I just want to do God's will, and He's allowed me to go up to the mountaintop, and I've looked over. And I've seen the promised land!!"*

Although this Baptist preacher claimed the Christian Scriptures as his fundamental guide, it was the imagery of the Hebrew Scriptures that really held him, and held the rest of us. He understood his work under the image provided by Exodus—of leading his people on a *new* crossing of the Red Sea. He is a Moses who goes to the mountaintop and looks over, but who is not privileged to enter with his people into the promised land. And while Biblical imagery was profound in King, he was still able to reach beyound it. He drew deeply from the Gandhian image of the "Satyagraha"—the nonviolent truth-force. And he appropriated the profound image of American civil religion at its best and noblest; the image of a land from whose every mountainside freedom would ring; the image of a dream come to reality.

We remember what these life-giving, life-enriching and extending images did for our national psyche. We understood the rich light they cast upon us as people. And for those who were so out of touch with the times that they could not understand the ennobling image there remained nothing but psychic damnation. The TV program *First Tuesday* reported that Martin Luther King's funeral in Atlanta was thickly attended by agents of the F.B.I. With their customary resourcefulness, some agents were inside the church relaying the proceedings by walkie-talkie to other agents outside. An agent inside reported that Mrs. King still expected the dream of her husband to be fulfilled. Back came the rather worried radio instruction from command central to "Find out what that dream was!" Psychic damnation.

The dream of a King and the dream of a Duke. Each dream is capable of harnessing the reflected light of powerful images. But both the Klan and King seem remote to us today. We are not crossburners or night riders, nor do we see ourselves as prophets and liberators. We deplore the one and admire the other, but truly identify with neither. The claim which each exercises upon us is more academic than existential. But the truth is that vivid extremes are often the only things that can give definition to those blurred gray areas that are still not in focus. King and the Klan are both vivid extremes, flashes of lightning giving definition to blurred gray areas of our society and of our lives lived in this society.

David Duke and the KKK are reminders of our capacity for lethargy; for ignoring the struggles going on around us; for our all too ready willingness to accept as a "given" the fact that African Americans remain the group most negatively affected by inflation, joblessness and urban decay.

Martin Luther King and the Civil Rights movement remind us of the best in ourselves and our society, which we are called to support and amplify. Freedom is indeed "a constant struggle." Rev. King showed us that participation in that struggle is life giving, life affirming, life changing work by which we ourselves experience liberation. Rev. King awakens us to the joyful creation occurring within us when we commit ourselves to building the human into humanity. He believed we could live our lives in accordance with his vision. African Americans and black persons the world over, from Selma to Southern Africa, continue to believe it and continue to demand it of us. It is possible! We can do it! We *shall* overcome!

# FASCISM, RACISM, AND THE KLAN

Fix in your mind's eye an image of a storm. This storm is peculiar to India and south Asia. A monsoon. While I have not experienced a monsoon directly, I have read and heard accounts by those who have done so, and I am profoundly impressed by the storm's ferocity and by the drama that anticipates its arrival. A monsoon is always preceded by a period of waiting. You wait for days, weeks. You wait in the knowledge that something is coming, something is going to break the peaceful, sun-baked atmosphere. Then on a given day the sky starts to cloud over. You can see the clouds approaching from a long way off. With the coming of the clouds a high wind develops, preparing the way. Then there is silence. Perhaps as long as an hour when nothing stirs. During that time the village gods seek shelter and the leaves of the acacia trees droop in the absolute stillness. The sky turns a kind of yellow. Then the raindrops. Large, pellet-like drops begin to fall. Sheet after sheet of rain, propelled forward by an incredible wind that has the power to sweep whole villages away in its fury. The rain and the wind continue for weeks and weeks.

During the decade of the 1980s we experienced the first stages of a political and social monsoon. And we worry lest we not pay attention to it before it engulfs us all. I think it is terribly important to identify this threat, to call it by its right name, and not to confuse the storm with the variety of harbingers signaling its coming, just as it would be inappropriate to confuse the individual raindrops with the torrents of rain that accompany the storm.

The monsoon which I want to hold up and consider is American "fascism." Its fundamental component, the wind driving it forward, is "racism." The harbinger of its coming, those first large raindrops striking our society, are American Nazis and the Ku Klux Klan.

123

The storm is not the Moral Majority, those noisy, self-righteous, sanctimonious folks, although the Moral Majority may very well be caught up in it. The storm is not the 50,000 so-called "Survivalists" with their brass-knuckle rhetoric, who want to huddle in bunkers and wait out the apocalypse, although Survivalists will probably be caught up in it. The storm is not Ronald Reagan, who made the extraordinary statement that "There are worse things than to be at peace." And yet, Reagan may well be caught up in it. The storm is not George Bush or even Dan Quayle, who promise a "kinder, gentler nation" and assure that minority poor folks remain precisely that: poor minorities.

The storm is gathering in all its component parts. This gathering storm is most clearly perceivable in what happened in that courtroom in Greensboro, North Carolina, a decade ago, when the Klu Klux Klan and the Nazis were acquitted of the slaying of five Communist Workers Party members. Four of the five Communist Workers Party members were white. Three of them were medical doctors and one was a graduate of Harvard Divinity School. An all-white jury acquitted the Klan and Nazis after the entire nation watched television coverage on November 3, 1979. If you were watching that evening you saw the Klansmen and Nazis drive up to an anti-Klan demonstration, open car trunks, remove weapons, deliberately pass them out to each other, check them to see if they were loaded, and fire them at the demonstrators point-blank. All on camera! And the defendants were found innocent! It was not the front-page news it should have been, and many people outside Greensboro, North Carolina discarded the incident as part and parcel of what occurs below the Mason-Dixon line.

To discard or disregard the importance of the Greensboro occurrence is elitist, foolish and dangerous. The coalition of the Klan and Nazis in Greensboro had the amazing candor to identify itself quite correctly as the "United Racist Front." How many organizations are involved in the United Racist Front is not known. But the fascist threat they represent is abundantly clear in both an historic and contemporary context.

In Germany the 1920s corollary to the Klan was the Nazi Militia, the Brown Shirts. The Brown Shirts and their allies halted a German move toward Socialism, a movement which had been developing since before World War I. The National Socialist German Workers' Party, the Nazis, utilized the Brown Shirt paramilitary squads and conquer promajor capitalists to intimidate, divide and conquer proSocialist forces that were operating in Germany during the 1920s.

The Greensboro scenario is a paradigm for the fascism operating in our country. Murder and overt violence with subsequent community acquittal and acquiescence demonstrates that fascism is alive, well, and increasingly acceptable. It has satisfactorally tested the waters of public opinion in various U.S. locations to see if they are congenial to it, to see if they will nourish this kind of virulent disease, and to see where to place long term initiative and money. The use of isolated violence, covert organizing, secret political influence and money are the URF-Klan tactics. They were also Black and Brown Shirt tactics.

There is big money and big political support for the activities of the fascist/racist front. Exhibit A: Jesse Helms, Senator from North Carolina, defender of Taft-Hartley anti-labor laws, key supporter of the World Anti-Communist League which was born out of the ashes of Nazi Germany. The League consolidated an unholy alliance with the Liberty Lobby, the American Security Council, the Young Americans for Freedom, the Asian People's Anti-Communist League of Taiwan, and on and on. Having such a good friend in such a high place is not the only component of that racist attack in Greensboro. The participating Klansmen and Nazis had weapons; they had a paramilitary organization; they had support from the police force that told them exactly where the anti-Klan demonstration was going to be; they had the ideology of racial supremacy; they had the support of business leaders. Add to these local circumstances the national climate of anger and the conditions contributing to that anger: economic depression, rising unemployment, double digit inflation. Add to these: access to media (e.g., Christian Broadcasting Company) as an avenue where the grievances of those who see themselves as dispossessed can be aired regularly, or where conservative Christianity can pave the way for white Christianity to influence, then run, Washington.

It's all there! All of the elements that combined to produce the Brown Shirts in Germany in the 1920s and 1930s. All of the elements creating American fascism today. The storm clouds thicken and move in. Anyone who has ever organized a Pro-Choice rally, or held an ERA demonstration, tangled with the nuclear industry, or protested the reinstitution of draft-registration knows the forces of fascism are there and are gaining in strength.

The storm is fascism. Its fundamental component is racism. Its harbinger is the Klan.

What is fascism? I think it is important to separate its meaning from the emotional "heat" the word's use generates. "Fascism" is not simply every group that is ugly and violent. "Fascism" is not simply violence. It is not simply the Nazi Party or the Klan, or other movements proclaiming a gospel of racial supremecy. The common definition of Fascism in Germany in the 1920s and 1930s is a definitive one, which we have forgotten at our peril. "Fascism" is the intervention of the state to save capitalism. That is the definition of fascism that is really historically measurable. The intervention of the state to save capitalism by capitalists who are running the state. Such a definition is historically measurable in that one can turn to the history of Mussolini's intervention to save the tide of capitalism in Italy in the 1920s or Hitler's alliance with the German Chamber of Commerce and the National Association of Manufacturers in the 1920s and 1930s. Closer to home, we can speculate about the government's interest in saving Lockheed and Chrysler Corporation.

When the state uses its power to prop up private corporate enterprise, it is a relatively short step for the state to start using coercive power to break trade unions, (witness Reagan and the air traffic controllers' union), to threaten opponents of private enterprise (witness government tactics against homeless and health plans), and to impose economic and social restrictions for which disobedience can result in jail (witness moves for AIDS registration and threats to Gay and Lesbian organizations).

That is fascism! Historically measurable and identifiable. It is fascism in Chile. It is fascism in South Korea. It is fascism in Brazil. It is fascism in El Salvador. And it is fascism in Greensboro, North Carolina. Except in Greensboro, it is covert, hidden and disguised as "just good ole boys"— penny-dreadfuls parading with white sheets over their heads. But we must bear in mind continually that under the hoods, behind the spray can slogans, distributing racist literature, burning crosses on property of black renters and homeowners, the fascist Klan is reviving.

The Klan's appearance and re-appearance in American history occurs at times of social and economic turmoil. In 1979 the Klan had a bumper year for their activity. There were cross burnings in Oklahoma, there were rallies in Connecticut, there was recruiting in public high schools in Massachusetts. The Anti-Defamation League states that, "Although there may be only 10,000 card-carrying Klanspersons, they have 100,000 sympathizers." As the League says: "While the KKK still speaks for only small segments of the American population, that segment is growing proportionately larger every day." With the Reagan administration, support for the Klan and its fascist components took a quantum leap.

I used to think that the KKK was an anomaly, an aberration of our national social policy. I now reject such thinking. The prime element about the Klan is that throughout its history, throughout its several incarnations, mutations and transmutations, it has never been an aberration. It has always been a functioning part of the American system, playing an important role in helping the system go. In a sense, the Klan is the system: this has never been more pointedly or succinctly stated, than by Skip Robinson, leader of the United League of Northern Mississippi: "The Klan that wears the white robe is merely the tool of the Klan that wears the three-piece suit."

This truth was underscored for me by the Unitarian Universalist minister, The Rev. Philip Zwerling, in a 1985 sermon commemorating the death of Bill Sampson, who was murdered by the Klan in Greensboro. Zwerling commented that while some of us speak out against the Klan, the strategy in so doing has been incomplete. We have treated the Klan as a peculiarity rather than as an integral part of a larger system, functioning on behalf of the system. The Klan and other fascist groups are a tool, an instrument of repression to be used and discarded by those in power, to be employed when people in power need it and tossed away when they do not need. it.

The KKK's history reflects the story clearly. It was organized in 1865 and used to deflect the whole force of reconstruction. It was used to maintain and defend Jim Crow. It was used to fight integration. It is used today to bolster and support the country's drift to the right, the drift toward increased imperialism and military muscle flexing, the drift toward ever more repressive legislation.

A storm of monsoon proportions is gathering. Its name is fascism. The vehicle carrying it forward is racism. Its harbinger is the Klan and other related White Power racist groups. What can we do?

There are two things we can do. We can remember that a fundamental component of religious commitment relates to concern for society's victims. Individually and collectively we can re-commit ourselves to keeping victims visible. That means that we can individually and collectively express our willingness to hear the pain, the anguish, and the anger of those who continually need to cry out for justice in our society. Our need to hear, see and respond to the victims is going to become more acute in the last decade of this century. We will need to be more discerning, more vigilant, because society's victims are going to disappear or, more accurately, they are "being disappeared" by the system. They disappear in a welter of public relations announcements issued by the various bureaucracies—local, state, national and international.

When I made that comment to a gathering of clergy, one replied, "I think that is a terrible overstatement." Two weeks later one of President Reagan's spokespersons announced that there was no longer any poverty in the U.S.! Poverty had disappeared, by Government proclamation. This will continue. Victims will disappear—no more poverty, no more people. Victims will vaporize under government statistics or social blame.

So the first thing we must do is to keep the victims visible. The second is that we must continue to hold up a vision of ultimate possibility. A vision that is so compelling that it can sustain us in our present situation. A vision of justice and purpose and possibility for all, sufficient in its power to shape our dreams and awaken us from our nightmares.

There is no single authorized version of this vision, nor should there be, because what matters, as Paul Tillich once pointed out, is that there is a power from which the vision of human fulfillment and just society is derived. Not merely the power of analysis but the power within each individual being that presses toward new fulfillment beyond the disunity into which it has fallen.

We live in deeply troubling times. In churches, synagogues, temples, assemblies, in houses of worship, we light candles. We light candles at Hanukkah, at Christmas, at times of celebration, and at times when there seems to be nothing to celebrate. This is important because the flickering of a candle like the power of an individual life or a single initiative carries an intense, brilliant illumination. We may not know if that "light" is merely the light of a candle or the light of a blazing sun. We do not need to make that distinction. Whether it is a candle or a blazing sun is secondary to the fact that the light shines!

# THE COURAGE OF
# OUR CONTRADICTIONS:
## Perspective on a Time of Trauma

"With the decision in 1970 to end the funding of the Black Affairs Council (BAC), all effective Unitarian Universalist Association attention to racial justice ended too," observed then Unitarian Universalist Association Vice President, William Schulz, in his preface to The Rev. Mark Morrison-Reed's study, *Black Pioneers in a White Denomination.*[1] Rev. Schulz was correct in this assessment. During the 1970s the denomination turned its attention to empowerment of women, gays, the elderly and the young, preferring to ignore and bury in its collective psyche the negative feelings which the Black Empowerment Controversy had generated. But those feelings resembled unruly guests, who, having interrupted the decorum of a sedate house-party and been summarily ejected from the premises, sneak back to take up residence in the basement of the house. From that locale they send disquieting signals of their continued presence to the dignified assembly in progress above stairs.

A decade after the divorce of BAC from the Unitarian Universalist Association, the Board of Trustees authorized the conduct of an Institutional Racism Audit, with the Association itself the object of inquiry.[2] The Audit was conducted by Community Change, Inc., in conjunction with a Unitarian Universalist Association Internal Audit Team. In the course of its inquiry, the Audit Team noted the frequency with which the topic of the Black Empowerment Controversy arose. Repeatedly the Controversy and the feelings which it had generated were offered as reasons for the denomination's failure to deal with the issues of racial justice. Noting the Unitarian Universalist preference for talking, if not as a substitute for action, at least as a way of postponing action for as long as possible, one of the Audit Team members observed that while Unitarian Universalists were willing and eager to discuss the Controversy on a rational and theoretical level, they exhibited great reluctance to state their *feelings* about what had happened. This led the observer to note, "The history of leftover feelings becomes a part of today."[3]

The Audit went on to inventory what the team identified as "leftover feelings." Those included anger, discouragement, suspicion and frustration, feelings which the Audit Team pointed out continue to encumber white Unitarian Universalists and black Unitarian Universalists in their attempts to create authentic relationships.

The "leftover feelings" originate from unresolved conflicts within the structure of contemporary Unitarian Universalism. The Black Empowerment Controversy did not create these conflicts. The Controversy did serve to strip away some of the veneer that had obscured them. Our collective failure to confront the Black Empowerment Controversy, or to identify the factors that prevent us from achieving a balanced assessment of its impact, reflects a reluctance to confront our own middle-class acceptance of that posture. Some of the negative feelings ostensibly generated by the Controversy can be traced to an attempt to 'blame the messenger who brings the bad news.'

The ideological "bad news" becomes apparent from an examination of the following areas: our inability to understand or to generate sympathy for the nature and purpose of "mission" or "missionary activity;" our failure to perceive the revolutionary nature of participatory democracy; our reluctance to confront racism's influence upon white as well as black people; our refusal to subject the concept of guilt to institutional application; our inability to distinguish between judgment as punishment and judgment as a means of grace.

Unitarian Universalists have historically abjured the idea of "mission," defined as the propagation of the faith to those who lack awareness of it and who might benefit from its acquisition. Our failure to engage in "missionary" activity has marked a significant difference between Unitarian Universalists and the main body of the Christian Church, which has regarded such activity as one of its main tasks from the very beginning.

Our denominational rejection of missionary enterprises has been based on the conviction that such an enterprise reflects paternalistic arrogance and theological imperialism, which do not harmonize with our Unitarian Universalist principles of religious self-determination.

In truth, we have demonstrated our own brand of arrogance in our failure to understand the meaning of the missionary enterprise in terms other than caricature or one-way street. While correctly abjuring the role of the "white missionary bringing the good news to the black downtrodden," we have failed to understand the sense of identification with those in need and the gifts resulting from solidarity which underlies most missionary enterprise in the twentieth century.

Black people who come into this essentially white middle-class denomination discover the presence of the same kind of white arrogance that has been a part of Western civilization's style of life. When they look closely at us they see this arrogance evidenced in the way we have responded to the inner city; they see it asserting itself in our theological schools; they see it exhibited in our ability to give but not to receive. And the arrogance overwhelms any suggestion that radical change in the process might be beneficial to our denominational health.

After citing numerous instances of this arrogance in the treatment meted out to the black pioneers who sought to make their considerable gifts available to the Unitarian denomination, Mark Morrison-Reed concludes:

> "The Unitarian church was not integrated because it chose not to be...Paternalistic in their racism, our leaders in the beginning of the twentieth century did not respect the black man. Slowly, over a period of decades, some Unitarians began to see their way out of this, but it was still difficult to break the patterns of

*segregation that were demographically and socially perpetuated.*"[4]

A significant component of our failure to accept and support the initiatives of the Black Unitarian Universalist Caucus/Black Affairs Council (BUUC/BAC) stemmed from our failure to perceive it in the context of "mission." Denominational leaders were not prepared; nothing had prepared them to understand the concept of empowerment or the virtue of enabling people to develop their own style rather than become imitators of our prevailing white middle-class style. Denominational leaders were not prepared to express the radical critique (again the missionary critique) that the orderliness of our religious lifestyle (expressed both in our worship and in our conduct of business) covered selfishness, narrowness and support for perpetuation of the status quo. Denominational leaders were not prepared to ackowledge that even as BUUC/BAC was dealing with and accepting funds from the white power structure of the denomination, its first allegiance was to the black community. BUUC/BAC's goal was to make the black community and its lively power a conspicuous reality for a denomination that had scant previous knowledge or understanding of that community's existence or leadership.

Few within this denomination had sufficient involvement with the black community to understand or appreciate the significance of BUUC/BAC as "mission"—a way to bind in solidarity with the oppressed on the one hand, and provide us with a radical and healthy critique of our own values and structures on the other.

Writing on this controversy, Mark Morrison-Reed acknowledged that while we as a denomination had taken leadership in responding to the Black Revolution in 1967 and 1968, we "quickly stumbled and fell, while at least one denomination which was slower to respond to the rebellion but had active mission in urban areas since the 1950s strode past us."

The church referred to is the Reformed Church of America. Noel Erskine's study, *Black People and The Reformed*

*Church in America*,[5] provides a detailed account of the formation of the Black Council of the Reformed Church of America and of its impressive and lasting response to the Black Revolution. The most significant difference between the Black Council of the Reformed Church of America and BUUC/BAC of the Unitarian Universalist Association is that a ready avenue of communication with the denomination was already in existence in the Reformed Church, in the form of perhaps 25 inner-city churches which were predominantly black churches and embodied a black style of worship and a black consciousness. These churches acted as buffers and conduits, serving to soften the impact of black rhetoric falling upon essentially white ears on the one hand, acting as avenues for those ideas and programs and perspectives to gain entry and acceptance into the wider Reformed Church community on the other.

Rather than continuing and working to strengthen Unitarian Universalist inner-city churches which were struggling (and continue to struggle) with changing conditions and demographic shifts, Unitarian Universalists largely abandoned these churches. We preferred to follow the white Unitarian Universalist flight to the suburbs. Whereas in the City of Boston there existed up to forty Unitarian or Unversalist churches at the turn of the century, there are seven today. The Unitarian Universalist Association Department of Extension has only recently determined the appropriateness of aiding the inner-city urban churches that remain.

The Rev. Morrison-Reed charges that BAC was "ready to dole out money to its needy clientele—but not to engage creatively its religious partners."[6] The history of the controversy from 1967 to 1970 reveals an extraordinary degree of creative engagement at all levels. The main factor was not lack of engagement, but that engagement was limited to personal and group encounters without benefit of institutional mediating structures (mission communities) which might have provided the leaven, such as served the Reformed Church of America so well in its dealings with black power.

Democratic process is commonly ackowledged to be the primary Unitarian Universalist methodology for "unearthing the truth." As The Rev. Daniel Higgins stated, "Our salvation lies in our willingness to be open and receptive to our chosen methodology."[7] In his critique of the Black Empowerment Controversy, Rev. Higgins charged that, "when Unitarian Universalists engaged this social issue...they abandoned their theological method. They bowed down to Baal and sacrificed their methodology to the god of relevance."[8] The impression given is that the controversy was something alien to and outside of Unitarian Universalism, demanding that we abandon our principles in order to engage in it, rather than an internal issue radically affecting our self-perception and demonstrating that we had not appreciated the radical nature of the very democratic principles we avowed. Rather than abandoning our democratic methodology, black Unitarian Universalists pointed out that we had never fully acted upon our precepts, since we had heretofore seen fit to exclude them from meaningful leadership roles.

One of the lessons to be learned from the encounter between black and white Unitarian Universalists is that the democratic process is essentially an encounter among people with differing interests, perspectives, opinions—an encounter in which the people reconsider and mutually revise opinions and interests, both individual and common. This encounter happens always in a context of conflict, imperfect knowledge, uncertainty. The conflict resolution achieved is always more or less temporary, subjected to reconsideration, rarely unanimous. What matters is not unanimity but discourse between equally empowered persons or groups. The fact that black Unitarian Universalists had no established and generally recognized power base called the democratic enterprise into question.

The democratic method affirms that only in political struggle can we recognize that the conditions under which we live are the result of human creation (and not the result of some given supernatural order). These conditions change as humans beings change. Change occurs in the context of political struggle. In political struggle we take charge of our history-making abilities.

It was this affirmation of the democratic method in all its radical nature that empowered not only Unitarian Universalist black persons but also Unitarian Universalist youth to assert their needs and their unique perspectives during this period. They were met in their effort by those who, while giving lip service to democratic process, did not perceive its radical nature; who operated in the implicit belief that hierarchy, bureaucracy and established expertise make sense, and that those who would reshape the denomination in radical ways must adapt to requirements.

One day, as Albert Camus wrote, "a slave who has been taking orders all his life suddenly decides that he cannot obey some new command, and he says, 'No More.'"[9] Such a declaration occurred at the 1967 Emergency Conference in New York City between black Unitarian Universalists and their denomination.

Historically, popular empowerment has appeared not only on the large, dramatic scale of revolution but also on the small everyday and local scale of a denominational conference. Not only in the Russian, French and American Revolutions but also in the struggles of the Civil Rights movement and the Women's Movement. It can begin with a small incident (on a bus in Montgomery, Alabama or in a hotel room in New York City) and spread to mobilize a nation or a denomination (or the world).

What occurred within our Unitarian Universalist ranks was not a rejection of democratic method but a revolutionary demand that it be put into practice. Our denomination was simply the context for one more chapter in a relatively familiar recurring story: the persistent struggle pursued in the widest variety of ways, under the most diverse circumstances, of people finding ways to participate in the decisions that affect their lives—decisions from which they have been excluded by the formal institutions of power.

If we place the Black Empowerment Controversy in the

context of a listing of historical examples of efforts to enlarge the scope of participatory democracy, another truth is revealed. None of the examples could be said to have succeeded unambiguously. However, successful outcome is not the only measure of a movement's significance. Even though the black empowerment controversy did not succeed in changing the power structure and the power brokerage practices of the Unitarian Universalist Association, it provided an example of how an institution and its membership could be guided to democratic directions.

Charging that the tactics of black separation were in violation of the democratic process (our theological method), Rev. Higgins continued a long-standing misapplication of theology to the concept of racial integration. Until the mid-1950s, American theologians (both black and white) had taught that social progress and the unity of humanity depended upon the disappearance of all ethnic and racial identity and separateness. It was liberal religious dogma that the closure of sociological and spiritual space between races would eventually achieve nonsegregated churches and a nonsegregated society. "What though the Kingdom's long delay and still with haughty foes must cope, it gives us that for which to pray, a field for toil and faith and hope," we said and we believed.

That racial identity should be no bar to full fellowship and participation in church or society, we had made very clear. Where we were mistaken was in the supposition that white perceptions of human reality in American society and in our Unitarian Universalist churches were the (acceptable) qualified liberal democratic perception. We did not fully appreciate the role that white racial identity (and its identification with the dominant racial values of this society) played in our perception of reality.

Black humanity in America has been formed in the matrix of psychological and physical suffering, segregation, discrimination and the ever-present remembrance of a previous condition of involuntary servitude. Out of this condition have come human beings whose sensibilities and

137

perceptions, religious and secular, are rarely identical with those who are "born and raised white" in America. This does not invalidate black sensibilities and perceptions. Quite the contrary, they provide a necessary balance and corrective to the perception of white America. The African American experience enables the bearer of that experience to discern in the workings of the democratic method elements that most white liberals have forgotten and ignored.

To the extent that Unitarian Universalists (and the white American religious community in general) ignored or denigrated African American sensibilities and perceptions, by presupposing that the themes and motifs of an "integrated" (read "desegregated, but white") denomination were normative for all Unitarian Universalists, Unitarian Universalism disqualified the African American perspective as effectively as black people had been disqualified by white politicians, white labor leaders and white business enterprises.

The rise of the Black Power movement after 1966, with its emphasis upon black solidarity, pride and self-determination, completed the destruction of integrationism as the dominant ideology of the black community *but not of the white community.* Throughout the period which we have been considering, the theological defense of integration did not lack spokespersons who, in their zeal, failed to take into account the painful deracination and dehumanization which African Americans were called upon to suffer as the price of a powerless and humiliating assimilation into an essentially racist white middle-class liberal denomination and culture.

A critical, ethical issue raised by the Black Empowerment Controversy revolved around the question of guilt. Throughout the Controversy those who were opposed to the denominational funding of BAC charged those who supported the funding of being "guilt-ridden" and of attempting to transpose denominational guilt into support of the Black Agenda. Accusers cited the fact that the Cleveland General Assembly in 1968 occurred only six weeks after the assassination of Martin Luther King, Jr., during a time of liberal

138

grief and remorse.

There is no question that the assassination had affected supporters of funding BAC at Cleveland, as it had affected American society generally: the assassination was the supreme statement of racism's corrosive effect and the ultimate measure of the failure of the nation to create a humane and equitable society for white as well as for black people. The assassination of Rev. King symbolized how, on the level of power, racism is used to effect magical solutions of unresolved social problems of the white community. But this awareness of the structural and institutional significance of the assassination was not generally shared within the denomination, which reflected the standard middle-class understanding of guilt expressed totally in individualistic terms.

Our middle-class society is imbued with the spirit of individual piety. Because of this emphasis upon individualism and personal responsibility for one's acts the singular person is isolated from owning significant responsibility for the social structure. The individual is encouraged to concentrate his/her moral energies on personal and interpersonal areas. The result is a feeling of being divorced from and having no significant responsibility for a society in which African Americans are oppressed and black leaders assassinated. The individual feels detached from and not responsible for the evils inherited from the past or for the generally oppressive structure of the present social system. Guilt and innocence are treated as personal feelings (if one doesn't *feel* guilty, then one is *not* guilty). Lack of guilt feelings is taken as sufficient evidence of innocence. Statements indicating a guilt that is not individually felt or acknowledged as one's personal responsibility are suspect. They are interpreted as betokening an ulterior motive or personality dysfunction.

Although personal guilt feelings were largely absent, there did exist throughout the denomination a sense that we should have overcome the structured dimensions of racism in our society, woven into the very fabric of our middle-class culture. While not personally guilty of slavery, lynchings, or other past systematic human degradations based upon race, all white people living in the society are guilty of allowing the residue, the sublimation, and the consequences of those racist degradations to persist in our institutions.

Drawing upon his experience in Germany, Professor James Luther Adams makes the point that, "Post-Nazi Germany provides us with a warning. In some quarters in Germany, the memory of the Nazi period has elicited only rationalizations that aim to explain away the evils of Nazism and responsibility for them. In attacking and revealing these evasions of responsibility, the more healthy-minded Germans have asserted that the rationalizations are bound to leave Germany corrupt; indeed, make it more corrupt."[10]

Our past is still a part of the structure of the present. Not only is the past related to the present, but actual personal guilt (whether acknowledged or not) is inextricably bound up with the guilt of institutions which systematically exclude and deprive minorities. The problem is not how or whether we accept personal guilt feelings or, once accepted, how we deal with such personal feelings. The problem is institutional. At the center of the individual self there is a will, and the will can change. But is there anything in institutions comparable to the will that can be induced to change for the better?

If we view institutions, and particularly the liberal churches, as the product of social forces or the result of natural patterns of growth and decay reflecting social change, then the answer to the question must be negative. But social organizations are not simply the products of social pressures. To be a viable institution the organization must have an inner logic; it must have a claim to legitimacy that invests the network of relationships within it with a sense of purpose and a sense of worth.

In short, an institution is more than the sum of its parts. The question then is what shape will the institution take? The shape and the character depend upon what the institution is at its core and the place where the institution's basic values and purposes reside. These core values and purposes comprise the institution's spirit, or, more appropriately, its spirituality, its "soul."

African Americans have seen and made us aware that there is a core, a "soul" in institutions; middle-class Black Unitarian Universalists (having established an awareness of their blackness) made the rational, bureaucratic Unitarian Universalist Association aware of its "soul." How? By acting through BUUC and BAC to make the denomination cognizant of the contradictions which exist between honoring democracy as an organizing principle and acting upon its radical imperatives; by acting through BUUC and BAC to make us aware that integration (not merely as an attitudinal principle to be honored in our rhetoric but as a way of life to be practiced in the vast majority of our churches and fellowships) had not been effective in freeing us from the effects of our racism.

Black Unitarian Universalists had been sufficiently *included* in the Unitarian Universalist movement and were sufficiently familiar with Unitarian Universalist values and principles to be aware of the core, the "soul" of this religious institution. Black Unitarian Universalists had been sufficiently *excluded* to be able to identify the ways by which the Unitarian Universalist Association systematically but subtly denied and obscured and kept to itself the power of leadership and decision-making at its core. When Black Unitarian Universalists made their demands upon the institution the uncomprehending blankness of white faces was taken as evidence of an insidious attempt to sustain white power.

Black Unitarian Universalists could hardly be faulted for harboring such beliefs. Even a cursory reading of Unitarian Universalist history for more than a century leading to this conflict had acquainted them with the fact that Unitarian and Universalist prophetic voices had been calling churches and fellowships to new involvement in the transformation of modern life and a new awareness of the suffering of the oppressed in society. To the voices of the abolitionists were added the voices proclaiming the Social Gospel, women's

141

suffrage, child labor laws, the labor movement and the Civil Rights Movement. All of these had certainly occasioned intramural disputes and conflicts among Unitarians and Universalists, but the occasion for these disputes and conflicts was the continuing effort to get the liberal church to throw its weight on the side of justice. The Black Empowerment Controversy was another chapter in this ongoing story.

There is no question that the Administration of Unitarian Universalist Association President Robert West or the Unitarian Universalist Association Board of Trustees was relieved by the disaffiliation of BAC in 1970. The decision presaged a return to "normalcy" from the perspective of denominational leadership. Individuals, churches and fellowships would have the opportunity to support black empowerment directly through the purchase of BAC bonds, the means by which BAC proposed to fund the programs it had undertaken. But the denominational connection between BUUC/BAC and the Unitarian Universalist Association was at an end. Denominational leadership could content itself with the conduct of its regular business free from the pressures created by the Black Empowerment Controversy.

The divorce of BUUC/BAC from the Unitarian Universalist Association brought to an end the denomination's concern for racial justice. It also marked a serious decline in financial contributions to the denomination. Programs had to be curtailed; denominational departments had to be reorganized because of the financial situation. Not until another decade had passed would the Annual Fund rise to the level that it had attained (in the purchasing power of 1968 and 1969 dollars) during the turbulant years of the Controversy.

Even more debilitating to this liberal denomination was the exodus of black people from our ranks following the Controversy. Because no figures of church membership according to race exist, it is impossible to determine with accuracy the numbers of black Unitarian Universalists who left the denomination. Several observers opine that as many as one thousand black persons actually terminated membership in Unitarian Universalist churches and fellowships. Others who had not formally joined our denomination but who had observed with growing interest and enthusiasm the movement toward empowerment turned to look elsewhere for liberation initiatives.

The loss to our denomination is not limited to the loss of persons. In addition, we suffered the withdrawal of a unique and distinct perspective, a depth of understanding and a rich appreciation of the human condition that African Americans brought with them. While they were middle-class black people, they provided the denomination with the opportunity to discover first-hand that "the truth of freedom in the world is the truth of the truly disinherited and that the state of freedom is most accurately reflected in the lives of those at the bottom of society."[11] Following the divorce of BUUC/BAC from the Unitarian Universalist Association, these gifts of perspective would largely disappear beneath the surface of white middle-class ideology that would reassert its firm grasp upon Unitarian Universalism.

Whites as well as blacks left the denomination in the wake of the Black Empowerment Controversy. However, the decline in denominational membership has been linked to a number of factors and concerns. In addition to the denomination's involvement with BUUC/BAC and the black agenda, the escalating Vietnam War was proving to be a source of friction and stress.

Many persons who are close to an institution which is undergoing severe stress and inner turmoil wonder whether a house seemingly divided against itself can stand. They answer for themselves by getting out of the house. Others reach out to grasp modern society's propensity for technique in the belief that sufficient sensitivity training, administrative skill and conflict management can hold things together. Still others find that the moral legitimacy of the institution is severely compromised if not totally dissipated in situations of conflict, and they leave. While each of these responses found some favor with elements within Unitarian Universalism, none of them takes into sufficient consideration the durability of the institution or the enlivening power of its prophetic message.

The prophetic message is epitomized in a statement of Martin Luther King, Jr.: "If the church does not participate actively in the struggle for peace and for economic and racial justice, it will forfeit the loyalty of millions, because people everywhere will say that the church is paralyzed; but if the Church will free itself from the shackles of a deadening status quo and, recovering its great historic mission, will speak and act fearlessly and insistently in the cause of justice and peace, it will kindle the imagination of humankind and fire the souls of people, infusing them with a glowing and ardent love for truth, for justice and for peace."[12]

The Black Empowerment Controversy, 1967 to 1970, gave testimony of a church that did participate actively in the struggle for peace and for economic and racial justice. We can take pride in the fact that black Unitarian Universalists found this essentially white-middle-class denomination worthy of struggle and effort and involvement. We should take pride in the fact that we were the first denomination to vote a "reparational" amount of our denominational funds to the cause of black empowerment as defined by BUUC/BAC. By our General Assembly votes in 1968 and again in 1969 to fund the multi-racial Black Affairs Council, we were saying to African American Unitarian Universalists and to the black community generally, "Don't just take the money and go, but take us with you in a way that will contribute to a larger vision of a unified humanity for all of us, black and white alike."

But after the divorce of BUUC/BAC from the Unitarian Universalist Association we allowed ourselves to slip into "the shackles of a deadening status quo." We retreated into complacent arrogance as the denomination dwindled, urban churches closed, church school enrollment decreased, and the vital spirit of beneficent change in the area of racial justice moved away from us.

More than a decade later, the Black Empowerment Controversy remains buried below the surface of denominational consciousness, "a wreck" in the words of poet Adrienne Rich; a wreck demanding denominational recognition, exploration, retrieval.

> *I came to explore the wreck.*
> *The words are purposes.*
> *The words are maps.*
> *I came to see the damage that was one*
> *and the treasures that prevail...*
>
> *The wreck I came for:*
> *The wreck and not the story of the wreck*
> *The thing itself and not the myth...* [13]

The Black Empowerment Controversy has created its own mythology. Much of that mythology is negative; a "wreck" is not a subject that readily invites approval. The period with which we have been dealing did end in failure, with the denomination's leadership unwilling to provide the support mandated by the General Assemblies of 1968 and 1969.

Having taken the initiative among religious communities to honor the formation of a Black Caucus in our midst and to support black empowerment, we did fail to sustain the momentum of initial efforts.

And yet these failures should not obscure the hope and promise which BUUC/BAC's programmatic efforts and initiatives brought to the black community or the good will and interracial understanding that those programmatic efforts generated for Unitarian Universalism during a time when open hostility toward the racism of the white middle class was apparent.

The Black Empowerment Controversy left an aftermath of pain and frustration, tension and anguish, with which the denomination still must deal. But balanced against this negative residue, there is also a legacy of vitality and enthusiasm generated during the period of the Controversy and

145

reflected in the journals, fact sheets, newsletters, and broadsides which flowed from denominational presses. The flow dwindled to a trickle after the Controversy, as the denomination returned to bland standardization.

The period of the Controversy was "the best of times and the worst of times" during which we confronted our contradictions. We discovered that we were a denomination capable of great outpourings of energy and devotion as well as great constrictions of fear and anger. The contradictions which the Controversy generated remain largely unresolved. They continue to generate both pain and confusion.

Some measure of that confusion results from our failure to apply the concept of judgment to this period. Judgment as a prevailing condition is apparent in two contrasting reactions to the same event. Recalling the hours immediately following the assassination of Martin Luther King, Jr., one white Unitarian Universalist minister spoke of how the community in which he lived and served was gripped by a paralyzing terror. An atmosphere of profound immobilizing despair settled upon people. The society was collapsing, and there was nothing to be done. Another white Unitarian Universalist minister, attending a conference of FULLBAC ("Full Funding For the Black Affairs Council"), when the news of King's assassination was announced, was also profoundly affected. He recalls being gripped not by paralytic impotence and despair but by a sense of inescapable prophetic demands that the time for courageous action in the cause of racial justice was categorically imperative.

The assassination of King was, by any accounting, a judgment upon white middle-class society. A sense of having been tried and found wanting was manifest in our liberal religious community. But the two differing reactions to that sense of having been tried indicate the difference between judgment as deadening punishment and judgment as a positive, lifegiving, life-affirming summons to action.

The concept of judgment is often equated with punishment. This is a serious error. Punishment is not judgment but rather the result of judgment rejected; the result of one's refusal to accept responsibility which leads to isolation and despair. On the other hand, judgment accepted leads to a renewed sense of community; a sense of partnership with others who are struggling to right the wrongs of a society gone awry. Judgment accepted means admitting complicity in a grievous situation, accepting responsibility and feeling empowered to strive to correct that situation.

I have addressed and rejected a guilt thesis as inadequate to any but the most superficial understanding of the impact of the King assassination upon this period. As an alternative I suggest that the concept of judgment affords a positive assessment of the Unitarian Universalist denomination's achievements during the Black Empowerment Controversy without diminishing or demeaning the struggles undergone or the anguish experienced by those who shared and shaped this chapter in Unitarian Universalist history.

The Black Empowerment Controversy provided Unitarian Universalism with its most rigorous testing during this century. It demanded a width of imagination, a depth of sensitivity and a contagion of zeal. These are the marks of a religious transformation. No amount of high rhetoric or pious posturing can cover their absence. The Controversy transformed, and will continue to transform us as its meanings and resonances continue to impress themselves upon us. In all of the confusions, the angers, the tensions of that time it is possible to hear a new kind of rushing of the whirlwind of God.

# NOTES

1. Mark Morrison-Reed, *Black Pioneers,* Skinner House Books, Boston, MA 1980. Preface.

2. *Institutional Racism Audit,* Report to the Board of Trustees, Unitarian Universalist Association by Institutional Racism Audit Team and Community Change, Inc., April 1981.

3. *Ibid.,* p. 47.

4. Mark Morrison-Reed, op. cit., p. 146.

5. Noel Erskine, *Black People and The Reformed Church in America,* Reformed Church Press, Lansing, IL, 1978.

6. Mark Morrison-Reed, sermon delivered at First Universalist Church, Rochester, NY.

7. Daniel G. Higgins, "Color Line Controversy," unpublished manuscript, p. 17.

8. *Ibid.*

9. Albert Camus, *The Rebel,* New York: Random House, 1956, p. 13.

10. James L. Adams, "Our Unconquered Past," *Unitarian Christian,* 1967, p. 4.

11. Gustavo Gutierrez, *A Theology of Liberation,* New York: Orbis, 1973, p. 15.

12. quoted by James Lawson, "The Church and Direct Action," *Proceedings of the Second National Conference on The Church and Social Action,* Society for Common Insights, Vol. II, No. 2, Nov. 17, 1978, p. 31.

13. Adrienne Rich, "Diving Into The Wreck," *Poems, Selected and New,* 1950–1974, New York: Norton, 1974, p. 197.

# 6

## ...In The South African Crucible

# LIVING IN UNREALITY
## What the Whites of South Africa Don't See

From the hills above Cape Town you can see the penal colony Robben Island, an outcropping of rock in the middle of Table Bay. At the time of Robert Kennedy's visit to South Africa in 1965, Nelson Mandela was its most distinguished resident.

Flying into Cape Town, Kennedy told his pilot to circle low over the island and tip a wing in salute. Although white South Africans dismissed the gesture as "Kennedy panache," black South Africans were thrilled. So was I. Even a mere gesture acknowledging black South African leadership was encouraging to the blacks and whites working for social change with whom I identified myself.

During the 1960s I served as minister to a small, liberal, integrated Unitarian church in Cape Town and to two Unitarian fellowships in Durban and Johannesburg. To me, a white American, and to others, blacks and whites alike, Robert Kennedy was a symbol of white support for the civil rights campaign in the U.S. His visit came at a time when I still believed that white South Africans could be roused from their self-satisfied slumber and make the social changes necessary to accommodate black leadership. I was naive.

The white minority government was firmly committed not to accommodation but to repression. While I was in South Africa, people and organizations identified as posing a serious challenge to white rule were being outlawed. I served on the board of one such "radical threat," a fund established to provide legal counsel for political prisoners and support for their families. The fund was declared illegal and branded "a communist front." White South Africans who served with me on the organization's board were "banned," meaning that they were prohibited from meeting with more than one person at a time, from having their work published, and from being quoted in the press. I was informed by U.S. consulate personnel that the South African security police were suspicious of my continued presence in the country. In 1967 I chose to leave South Africa.

In the spring of 1985 I returned. I found that white South Africans were still as unwilling to listen as they had been a generation earlier. The message to the white rulers continued to be harsh: change or die. Rather than acknowledge that ultimatum, white South Africans retreat into their world and trust that the security forces will protect them from violence.

"We cannot permit violence," says a white Cape Town housewife, whose lifestyle is preserved by vigilant police and army patrols. Whites were all but unanimous in their praise of the police and soldiers involved in the shooting of 20 unarmed blacks who were walking in a funeral procession for slain blacks at Uitenhage in the spring. After the shooting, South Africa's minister of law and order lauded the action, saying that military units "must bear the brunt of attempts to destabilize South Africa" and that they were owed "a debt of gratitude and appreciation."

Meanwhile, life goes on as usual for white South Africans. Their suburban neighborhoods remain tranquil with nary a ripple from the growing violence outside to disturb them. The only blacks a white person in such a neighborhood sees are servants. It is not possible for whites to have social relationships with blacks unless they venture into black neighborhoods (townships), and to do that one must have a pass. Few whites apply for passes. Fewer enter illegally. However, I entered a number of townships in the 1960s and 1980s.

Whites I met during my visit remarked that I knew far more about what was happening in South Africa than they did. That is because the South African government sanitizes the news. Clashes between blacks and police are usually referred to in the news as "urban unrest." Police quell unrest with "tear smoke;" the government does not use the term tear gas. Why upset the citizenry with possible troubling connotations?

In the days following a massacre at Uitenhage, a black township near Port Elizabeth, white doctors who had been summoned to treat the shooting victims were instructed by police to save the buckshot slugs removed from black bodies and put them in containers marked with the victims' names. I asked a white political activist living in the area why this was necessary. She told me that the slugs thus identified could be used as evidence when the shooting victims were charged with the crime of having participated in an "illegal gathering." (Incidentally, the police call these slugs "bird shot," never buckshot. But if you hit a bird with one there would be nothing left but feathers.) My informant went on to point out that the white doctors were happy to comply.

White clergy in the area also cooperated with police demands including the demand that clergy not enter these hospital wards, even when some of those wards held shooting victims who had requested last rites.

The oft-repeated contention that white South Africans need to defend themselves against violence on their borders is absurd, given that white South Africa controls virtually all the country's powerful instruments of violence, up to and including nuclear weapons. An elaborate system of security measures, along with enforced geographical segregation, leaves black South Africans virtually no means for carrying on violent revolution beyond the confines of their particular townships or neighborhoods. A township resident told me, "God has given us our weapons: stones and petrol," but such "weapons" have little value beyond their capacity to provoke the awesome firepower of the security forces.

I was an eye-witness at one such David-and-Goliath encounter. Predictably, David lost. My wife and I had driven into the township of Zwide, near Port Elizabeth, in the Eastern Cape Province. The occasion was a funeral similar to the one held at Uitenhage two weeks earlier. During the morning the crowd grew from 10,000 to 30,000 blacks— always under police and army surveillance. The crowd sang and chanted. The names Nelson Mandela and Oliver

Tambo were shouted by youths who hadn't been born at the time of Mandela's imprisonment and Tambo's exile. At graveside thousands sang "Nkosi Sikileli Africa" ("God Bless Africa"), the anthem of the outlawed African National Congress.

And then the shooting began. Police and army troops, responding to raised fists and black-power slogans, opened fire on the crowd with tear gas, rubber bullets, and buckshot. I saw the tear-gas canister coming a moment before it smashed the windshield of my rented Toyota. Moving toward us was an armored personnel carrier, or "hippo," used by the South African police for crowd control in the townships. Police and soldiers were firing into the crowd around us. I spun the Toyota in a U-turn. Fleeing residents jammed into the car. We fled with the other township residents, who were running and leaping in every direction to escape the tear gas and the buckshot.

Within moments the frenzy subsided. People disappeared down small township side streets and alleys. One man carried another whose shirt was covered with blood. A young black man led us behind a cottage. A tent was pitched on the grass. It was hot and dim inside the tent. A youth and a child lay face down. Another teenager cut into the child's back with a razor blade and squeezed out a buckshot slug the size of my little fingernail. It was the first of three to be removed. Such backyard surgery is preferable to treatment at a local hospital and the arrest (accompanied by the charge of having participated in an illegal gathering) that would follow.

Next morning the state-controlled radio news broadcast minimized the encounter, reporting that one death had resulted from an incident of "urban unrest" in the township of Zwide. White South Africa was reassured that it had no cause for concern.

South Africa's white regime has created a security system that is the most organized, coordinated, and dedicated in the Western world. Experts have rated it tougher than the security systems of Israel and Northern Ireland. The coercive and repressive nature of its actions provokes criticism from the small liberal white community that still exists in South Africa.

Two decades ago, during the period I lived in South Africa, I believed that the ruling white society could find the intellectual and moral muscle to match its extraordinary tenacity. I thought that social transformation would eventually come about through white initiative. Twenty years later I've learned that I was wrong.

The recent past is replete with examples of white South Africa choosing cosmetic disguise over real social change, with results ranging from the absurd to the grotesque.

The South African constitution ostensibly provided the coloured (mixed race) and Indian populations of South Africa with voices in government. But the election of representatives from those groups to "a debating society" posing as a parliament was boycotted by 80 percent of the eligible voters in those communities. The election for black town councils (established to exercise control in the black townships) was boycotted by 90 percent of the black urban population. The violence vented against these black "puppets" of the white regime is horrifying evidence of this constitution's failure.

The repeal of the infamous sex-law legislation outlawing interracial marriage was hailed as a major step toward liberalizing South Africa. But, as persons of color were quick to point out, having the right to marry across racial lines is of small consequence in a society that continues to practice racial separation in housing, education, public transportation, and virtually every other potential avenue for social interaction between the races.

With the imposition of national "state of emergency" restrictions and regulations in 1985, even the pretense of accomodation was suspended. The "state of emergency" is part of a long series of legislative blunders that illuminate the fundamental legacy of apartheid: its unparalleled success not only in isolating white South Africans from those who share their country, but also in preventing them from achieving anything resembling a deep understanding of themselves. The Afrikaans poet Breyten Breytenbach sums up this isolation when he says that the white South African "has painted his windows white to keep the night in".

There is no possibility of a white-initiated social transformation in South Africa that would be acceptable to all South African racial groups. The most enlightened initiatives of P. W. Botha's and F. W. De Klerk's racist regimes have failed to meet the demands of the African National Congress and other significant opposition groups.*

The lengths to which white South Africa will go to preserve its isolation were reflected in its establishment of "tribal homelands," or "bantustans," as they were originally called. They represent white South Africa's "final solution," and their resemblance to the Nazi concentration camps does not end with that metaphor.

When I left South Africa in 1967 there was one established "homeland," Now there are ten. These homelands comprise a little more than 13 percent of the land of South Africa. Yet 28,660,000 black South Africans (85.3 percent of the population) are expected to call them home. They represent the culmination of the apartheid ideal that there be no black citizens in South Africa. In this scheme South African blacks are, as citizens of homelands, considered to be foreign nationals in South Africa at the whim of their white hosts, filling their host's labor needs and subject to discriminatory laws.

As they stand, the homelands serve to contain the political, economic, and social discontent that are the results of South Africa's stratified society. Conditions inside them go from bad to worse. As we travelled through backroads of one, the Ciskei, we could not fail to see raw poverty everywhere. In another "homeland," QwaQwa, a tiny under-

*The February 1990 release of Nelson Mandela represents a response to black South Africans' initiatives and world pressure. DeKlerk's response signifies a hopeful potential.

156

developed area of approximately twenty-five square miles, located in the remote reaches of the Eastern Free State, the population rose from 25,000 people in 1970 to 450,000, by estimate, in 1985.* Jobs within the area are almost nonexistent. Jobs within commuting distance of most "homelands" are insignificant. In QwaQwa there is profound suffering and widespread starvation.

The rulers of the homelands are increasingly called upon to enforce the policy of apartheid and to police the tensions it generates. The result is the creation of puppet dictators who boast their own private armies, networks of terror and oppression. These black leaders dominate their people with reassurance that they will be supported by white South Africa's military might.

I think of Lennox Sebe. Sebe rose quickly from the menial position of assistant inspector of Bantu education to become "life president" of the Ciskei homeland. He exercises unchecked political power without parliamentary opposition. He enjoys expensive cars, titles of office, overseas travel, banquets. He has appointed a number òf family members to high office; his brother, Major General Charles Sebe, is state security chief. Lennox Sebe has established close ties of cooperation with the South African security forces. His police and paramilitary squads of vigilantes repress dissent. In the Ciskei homeland Lennox Sebe reigns supreme.

Less extreme but no less menacing are the tactics and posturing of President Lucas Mangope of the Bophuthatswana homeland and Chief Gatsha Buthelezi of Kwazulu homeland. These leaders function with the blessing of the South African white government and the good will of the Reagan administration, without sign of change from the Bush administration. To varying degrees, all the homeland leaders rule with the whip. Buthelezi has been particularly

---

* The noted South African sociologist Frances Wilson reported the
   population reached 500,000 in 1990.

vocal in his attempts to persuade foreign businesses not to divest from South Africa. Moreover, he is known to be seeking to consolidate his power in the area he rules, the region around Durban. It was there, in the Phoenix settlement, that blacks massacred Indians and burned Indian homes in 1986. It seems likely that Buthelezi, at least tacitly, approved this action, which turned attention away from the struggle against white power.

Until the ban on reporting violence in the black townships that ring white South African cities, the media focused on the unrest in urban centers. Within the homelands, however, an even greater threat to peaceful social change continues: tyrannical life-presidents and super chiefs who resemble 20th century warlords trying to extend their territories or consolidate them with others. But as long as the ensuing violence is directed by blacks against blacks, white South Africa will ignore it. Like good Germans during the Nazi era, white South Africans show little concern for what occurs within their concentration-camp homeland system. How long white South Africa will be permitted to remain in self-imposed ignorance is an open question.

Two days before returning to Boston in 1986 I talked with Bishop Desmond Tutu. Tutu is a small man with a high voice and a quick laugh. I asked him to predict the future, and he responded with a derisive hoot. Then his expression changed. He recalled a scene at the funeral at Uitenhage for the massacred victims. Eighty thousand blacks crowded the sports stadium where the ceremony was held; fewer than two dozen whites were present. But among that handful was a family of four—a couple and their two children. While the mother breast-fed the youngest, the older romped with black spectators, to their mutual delight. Tutu recalled the scene with relish. "I want to believe that I was looking at the future of my country," he said.

Blacks, gathered to mourn violent deaths among their own people, still taking pleasure from the presence of a white child: a profound and compelling symbol. But is it the future? I would love to think so.

# SOUTH AFRICA: NAUGHT FOR YOUR COMFORT

A quarter of a century ago, before I first traveled to South Africa and began my ministry to Unitarian communities in Capetown, Johannesburg and Durban, I read Father Trevor Huddleston's book, *Naught For Your Comfort*, detailing the destruction of the black community of Sophiatown, located in what is now part of Johannesburg. The title is taken from a poem by Walter de la Mare which begins, "I tell you naught for your comfort, nor yet for your desire; but that the wind grows stronger yet and the sea rises higher."

Drawing upon his experience in Sophiatown, Huddleston made dire predictions about the future for South Africa, black and white. In the intervening years we have had more than indications of the violence implicit in that future. We remember the Sharpville massacre in 1960 and the brutal suppression of black South African students in the Soweto riots of 1976. Something else has happened in South Africa that makes Father Huddleston's bleak outlook all the more sobering and prophetic.

The difference between the present unrest (1985 to 1990) and previous outbreaks is that this time a critical threshold has been crossed. *Blacks know, suddenly, that they are going to win.* That is the writing on the wall—as prophetic as when the original writing recorded in the Book of Daniel, "Mene mene teckel parsin" appeared on the wall at Belshazar's feast announcing ruin! South African blacks don't know how long it will take, but they are confident that now they are on the last lap of their long liberation struggle.

What is going on now in South Africa is not a revolution in the classic sense of armed seizure of power. It is almost impossible to overthrow a modern industrial state as long as the police and the army stay loyal. And the police and the army are very loyal to the present white power structure.

But to that assertion should be added the fact that the security forces are in a no-win situation: the more they repress the black majority, the more they fuel the engines of revolution motivating and driving that majority.

Although the security forces of South Africa have formidable coercive resources at their disposal they cannot use them. For all their military might they cannot "nuke" Soweto. Short of such a destructive mechanism, all they can do is kill and detain more and more people (around 25,000 were detained in South Africa under the emergency proclamation of 1986). Killing and detaining is what they have been doing over the past thirteen years with a spectacular lack of success. The revolution will not be halted on the killing fields.

But what kind of a revolution is it that has South Africa in its grip? Perhaps it can best be described as a mighty upwelling of black rage that over years rather than over months will continue to sap and hemorrhage the racist power structure until that structure falls in upon itself.

The causes of this rage are well known to anyone who has paid even cursory attention to the South African situation over the past quarter of a century: the cumulative effect of generations of racial discrimination, almost four decades of distilled apartheid, the final exclusion of Africans from the new parliament that was created in 1984. Add to this growing unemployment, growing inflation and a myriad of local grievances.

But the turning point has been a *psychological* one in the black community. All the quantitative changes have added up quite abruptly to a qualitative change. Blacks have, for a long time, possessed the latent power to overthrow apartheid (there are more than 30 million Africans, "Coloureds,"* and Indians over against five million Whites, and the state is dependent upon their labor). But black South Africans have never before succeeded in mobilizing this power. Now, with the combination of increased black militancy and organization within South Africa, that time has come. Black South

*In South Africa "Coloureds" are persons of mixed black and white racial heritage.

Africans know they will win. It is true that "winning" is still in the future, but blacks know that victory will be theirs, and they know, in the words of Winnie Mandela, that "when we win, we will win forever."

Black morale is rising in South Africa while white morale is falling. While whites flounder, abandoning old solutions and groping for new ones, they continue to churn out new constitutions and cosmetic moves, while quarrelling and bickering among themselves. Blacks are angry, assertive, and sure of themselves. Whites are increasingly fearful, defensive, and uncertain about their future. Opinion polls taken in both black and white communities early in the 1980s register whites' fatalistic acceptance that apartheid will fail. In 1984 and 1985, white emigration *from* South Africa increased by 33 percent and immigration into South Africa decreased by 40 percent. The trend continued in 1986.

After the 1976 Soweto uprising over 4,000 black refugees fled South Africa. Unlike the youngsters in South Africa who fled during the Soweto uprising, black youths are not leaving now. They smell victory. While they know that the South African state is not going to be a pushover and that, indeed, it will be a long and bloody slog to their desired goal, they are ready for this with an almost reckless disregard for their own lives. As one observer of the scene has commented, "You have to be young to be so willing to die."

Blacks will be halfway to victory once they have established control over their own townships by making them ungovernable; to this end they have been ruthlessly eliminating agents of white authority: black policemen, counsellors, informers, and other collaborators with "the system" by harsh intimidation and, in some instances, brutal "elimination."

There is no question that the battle within the urban townships has become increasingly warlike. The ANC, which used to sabotage installations up and down the country with caution to avoid human bloodshed, has been smuggling its armory into the townships; automatic rifles, hand grenades, and limpet mines are part of their arsenal. White police and their black police lieutenants patrol the townships in armored vehicles (hippos), but as they do so the blacks melt into backyards only to reappear when the patrols have passed.

Each of the three main black groupings (African National Congress - ANC, Azanian Peoples' Organization - AZAPO, and Kwa Zulu's INKATHA) sense coming black victory; and, therefore, each of these groupings is positioning itself for the power struggle within the black community once victory is achieved.

The African National Congress (ANC) with its partner, the umbrella-like United Democratic Front (UDF), is supported by the new superfederation of black unions, the Congress of South African Trade Unions (COSATU). Affirming the principles of the 35-year old Freedom Charter, which calls for a multi-racial South Africa, the ANC reports the largest black power grouping in South Africa. The ANC is being challenged by a smaller but significant second group: Azanian Peoples' Organization (AZAPO). AZAPO with its partner, the National Forum, an organization of black consciousness bodies with some trade union support, is probably best identified as the successor of the Pan African Congress (PAC). The PAC has openly advocated black rather than multiracial rule for South Africa's future. The third major black grouping is that led by Chief Buthelezi and the massive movement based in the Kwa Zulu "homeland" called INKATHA.

Some observers believe that if peace cannot be made between Buthelezi and the ANC, South Africa will see, besides a white/black struggle, a black/black civil war.

Chief Buthelezi has accused the ANC of trying to assassinate him, and the ANC has countered with charges that Buthelezi's strongarm men are doing army and police dirty work. Black on black deaths have been a high proportion of the total deaths in current South Africa.

To the simpler minds in Pretoria, stifling an authoritative black African voice may seem to be a good way to maintain power. But it will be in the interests of whites in South Africa to acknowledge and look to a representative African voice. When that day comes, a representative African voice may not exist. With the banning of the African National Congress in 1960, the banning of 19 black consciousness groupings in 1977, and the banning of UDF leadership, the government prevented the emergence of black political parties.

For whites to draw comfort from this fragmentation in black ranks is dangerously shortsighted. Ranking Afrikaaner scholar Professor Hermann Giliomee has warned the whites that even more dangerous than the existence of a large black organization will be the absence of a large black organization. One day the whites will desperately need an authorative black government to create order out of chaos. It may very well be that on that day whites will search desperately among the fragmented black groups for that black voice and come up empty handed.

If there is fragmentation in the black society, there is also fragmentation in the white South African society. And the problem is similar: who will speak for whites with sufficient authority for negotiation? Suddenly the old fault lines and some new ones are surfacing in the white community. Between Afrikaans and English-speaking communities strains and tensions have always existed. To these traditional tensions must now be added the mounting confusion among whites, many of whom feel politically homeless.

The right wing of the white Nationalist Party has been in the ascendency during this decade. It has effected the resignation of President P. W. Botha, and the fall 1989 national (Whites, Coloureds and Indians) parliamentary elections. For years that right wing was seen as a lunatic fringe group whose members were political and social neanderthals who had failed to make the evolutionary leap from racial domination to reform. But now two new factors have resulted in gaining recruits for this right wing group: fear of the black revolution, on the one hand, fear that the white living standards will collapse overnight, on the other. This second fear is partly caused by the fact that the recession-stricken economy is unwinding and also because some expenditures on whites are being transferred under the present government to expenditures on blacks. Such conditions are viewed as intolerable by the white right wing.

Just as the military stepped into the political vacuum in the South African region, so they step into a political vacuum in South Africa itself, if politicians show themselves to be incompetent. It is significant that in 1986 when President P. W. Botha was negotiating with the "group of eminent persons" that had been dispatched from Britian to South Africa to find solutions for South Africa's racial problems, the South African military staged three raids simultaneously on three different neighboring countries. The object of such military action was twofold: to send a signal to the Botha regime that it had better not cut any deals, and to send a signal to the "group of eminent persons" about who is really in control of the situation in South Africa. The message was heard!

If the South African politicians do show themselves to be incompetent, no military coup will be necessary. The military and the police are an integral part of the security decision-making process. If the politicians falter, the military and the police will simply assert themselves more forcefully in their existing positions. White South Africa has exported terrorism worldwide. In 1987 ANC spokesperson Dulcie September was assassinated by a hit squad in Paris, France; a leading white liberal lawyer Albie Sachs was mutilated as the result of a car bomb in Maputo, Mozambique; in 1988 four ANC members were killed by a terrorist bomb at a home in Gabarones, Botswana; in 1989 well-known sociologist and political activist David Webster was gunned down in broad daylight on a street in Johannesburg.

The great cleavage in the white community is between those who know that radical apartheid reform can no longer be delayed and those who, confused and frightened, see the future as a fight for survival. The dynamics of reform have been out of phase with the dynamics of black aspirations. In the words of Winnie Mandela, "apartheid is a crime against humanity; you don't 'reform' a crime against humanity."

Is there a way out for South Africa? Yes! It has begun with legalization of black political activity and intense dialogue with nationally and internationally recognized black leaders. The longer an agreement to eradicate apartheid is delayed, the more black society will fragment and the more difficult it will be to negotiate a common settlement. *Cry the Beloved Country*, by Alan Paton, remains one of the most influential books ever written about the South African situation. In it one of the characters asserts, "My fear is that when your people have finally turned to loving, my people will have turned to hating." These are words which Paton put into the mouth of the black minister hero of this novel. As the situation in South Africa continues to unfold that sentiment seems prophetic. South African whites show little inclination toward loving to the degree that it involves surrender of their absolute power. South African blacks continue to struggle to affirm the Freedom Charter's ideas over against the forces within the black community calling for violent response to the violence of the white South African state. Nelson Mandela's release and his public rededication to the Charter's multiracial, democratic South Africa, governed by majority rule, has occurred none too soon.

The situation has been moving away from the vision of Alan Paton and toward the much more troubling image rendered by William Golding in his chronicle, *Lord of the Flies*. In that novel, children are marooned on a coral island. In their circumstances they create a barbaric society. In one memorable passage, the children are involved in a savage dance which leads to the killing of one of the boys. Golding writes, "A circling movement developed and a chant. While Roger mimed the terror of the pig, the little 'uns ran and jumped on the outside of the circle. Two of the boys found themselves eager to take a place in this demented but partly secure society. They joined the dance and the chant, 'Kill the beast. Cut his throat. Spill his blood.'"

165

I tell you, "naught for your comfort nor yet for your desire. But that the wind grows stronger yet and the sea rises higher."

# 7

# ...IN THE SELF

# TRUSTING THE PROCESS

Life is process, flow, movement; to live *well* one should sense the "movement," "go with the flow," "trust the process." Sage advice. Why do I have a hard time taking it?

Trusting the process is difficult for you, for me. There are times when I even have a hard time trusting the people who trust the process; they seem given to flowing robes and flowing emotions. I know myself well enough to know that given a choice between trust and control, a part of me wants to control. I want to control the process, or at least try to manage it. When someone tells me to trust the process, I become apprehensive. To voluntarily yield myself to the shifting and turning of events often strikes me as unfocused, irresponsible—and more than a little scary.

If my wary attitude resonates for you then we have something in common: our desire to control the future. Where we may differ is in the styles of control we choose. There are nearly as many different styles of attempted control as there are varieties of temperament. But they can be clustered into several categories.

The *bureaucratic* style. This is appealing if you are a logical, methodical, do-not-take-chances kind of person. You employ graphs, charts, statistics, task forces. You try to squeeze the future dry of spontaneous or novel juices. Life is reduced to technology. At least you are in control, and that's what you wanted, isn't it?

If the bureaucratic style does not fit, there is the *seductive* option. You control the future by charming others with an unceasing supply of smiles and good will. This style refuses to acknowledge conflict or opposition. You get your way (read: control) through limitless geniality.

Then there is the *paranoid* style. We had a president of the United States who was the very embodiment of this style. His eyes flashed this way and that as he held up his hands in "V" signs, with shoulders hunched protectively against a rear assault. The paranoid style operates from the assumption that any possibility for which we are not totally prepared will bring disaster. We spend much time fortifying the garrison future from which we can repel a sneak attack in the days, weeks, years ahead.

Closely allied with the paranoid style is the *gangbuster gambit*. Here the aggressive battler exercises control by grabbing the future and shaking it. The operational psychology can be summed up as "better-zap-them-before-they-zap-you." The style has a certain appropriateness in some occupations (e.g., if you are a pro football linebacker). But it is decidedly disadvantageous in most interpersonal relationships.

Finally, there is the *dependent* style. We become the friendly helper and facilitator. Those of us who are in the "helping" professions should be particularly aware of this style of control. We fill other people's needs solicitously, render them in our debt so that when they exercise their independence we can reclaim our hold with a variant on the age-old plaint, "After all I've done for you..."

Those are five styles of control by which we attempt to keep the future in a hammerlock. None works very well. All require substantial energy. But the alternative is to trust process! And that is not easy.

A story about a young Unitarian Universalist minister who was settled in his first full-time church reflects our dilemma. After he had been there for about two years he began to receive letters from other Unitarian Universalist churches expressing interest in him as a potential candidate for their pulpits. The young minister was flattered and yet indignant. He was happy in his parish, felt that more work remained to be done there, and had no intention of leaving the church in which he was happily located. He journeyed to denominational headquarters at 25 Beacon Street in Boston to ask why pulpit committees were contacting him. He was informed that his name was being placed on the pulpit committee lists.

"We thought that two years was long enough for you in the church which you are now serving. We thought you would be interested in moving," he was told.

"By no means," said the young minister. "I'm happy where I am." And then, in a fit of bravado, to which only very young ministers have ready access, he added, "The only church I would be interested in serving is the one located in Cape Town, South Africa!"

"Sorry," said the spokesperson in the Department of Ministry, "We have someone who is already committed to go there."

"Fine," said the young minister, "Then please do not put me on any more lists for at least a year or two." He returned to his parish.

A month later the phone rang in the young minister's parsonage. The Department of Ministry was on the line. After being apprised that the person scheduled to go to South Africa had developed a physical condition that prevented his going, came the question, "Were you serious about your concern to go?" The young minister called out to the young minister's wife, "Dear, do we want to go to South Africa?—for five years?" The young minister's wife replied, "Sure, why not!"

That was in 1962. My wife, our three-year-old son, and I went to South Africa with not much more forethought than I have conveyed here. It seemed the appropriate thing to do. We trusted the process that would carry us to South Africa, that would involve us in the profound currents and tides of that society and would change our lives in every conceivable way.

Use of words like "currents" and "tides" are appropriate in this context. Currents are associated with the flow of rivers and tides with the movement of oceans. Our lives resemble the flow of rivers subject to currents and eddies. There is a timing—a tide in our being and in our relationships—that we ignore at our peril. There is a flow and a movement of the human spirit. There is the natural unfolding of the initiatives of people. Even as we try (and some of us try very hard indeed) to cover every possible contingency, the "plans of mice of men gang aft aglee." The future comes with its own novelty and spontaneity. It outwits us with its newness and its unpredictability. In order to deal with it we need something better than a plan for all seasons. We need a deep confidence and a flexibility of the spirit that will enable us to trust the processes that carry our lives.

This trusting, accepting process is beautifully evoked in a book by John McPhee. Mr. McPhee writes for the *New Yorker* on all manner of topics—from the New Jersey Pine Barrens and the fish markets of New York City to the intricacies of hydrogen and how bombs are made of the stuff (*A Curve of Binding Energy*). Two of his essays were combined in a book dealing with the future of the birch bark canoe and the people who build these noble craft. I must admit that my own interest in birch bark canoes is marginal, and yet I was both captivated and deeply moved by McPhee's delightful discoveries. He speaks of a canoe trip and of his own personal astonishment when, while paddling, he discovered that the flow of the river was not against him but with and for him, and that it was possible for him to go with the flow of the river in confidence; that his own purpose could best be served by cooperating with the direction and movement of the current. For McPhee this knowledge, so simple and obvious on the face of it, carried all the impact of revelation.

When we come to truly believe that there is a flow in our lives, that the underlying currents moving in us and about us are not against us but are for us, that something of ultimate significance is literally in the flux and eddying motion of our hours and days, then it is possible for us to move with that flow in confidence that ultimate significance is with us literally in everything. Gradually, we may be able to accept the provisional character of the universe and of our lives.

It sounds so easy. And it is such a struggle. The struggle is movingly spelled out in the film *On Golden Pond*, which focuses on the fortieth summer (perhaps the last summer) of Norman and Ethel Thayer who have returned to their summer place on the shores of Golden Pond in Maine. Norman is a curmudgeon. An aging curmudgeon. When Ethel describes them both as middle-aged, Norman retorts that people do not live to be one hundred and fifty. Even though he can recognize the process of aging, he cannot trust it. He does not trust the process of relationships either—particularly with his daughter whom he will not allow to move beyond estrangement. He is scared to death of losing control over his life and uses nearly all the control techniques listed to maintain his grip. Of course, they do no good.

Norman is stalled within his "old" self. If he were allowed to·remain there, the film would be another dreary evocation of aging. But a teenage boy who is not cowed by Norman's controlling tricks succeeds in bringing the old man back to life. Norman comes to accept the provisional character of his life by the youth's reminder that his life is joined richly, deeply, lovingly with other lives—including his daughter. Thus Norman comes to trust the process of his dying and his living.

Psychoanalyst Erik Erikson asserts that the development of primal trust in the first year of a child's life is absolutely necessary for a child to grow into a healthy human being. The child must sense, first through the mother figure, then through other people, that there is a hallowed presence which can be depended upon, who cares, in whose everlasting arms she or he is okay, that everything is safe and well. That is how trust in the process begins and continues in ever-widening, ever-enriching patterns. To go with the flow of one's life is to live without a fixed blueprint or plan.

It is to be vulnerable to having your mind changed, your plans interrupted or discarded, your hopes dashed and your dreams unfulfilled. It is to trust that there is a goodness in the rapids of change as well as in the rocks of continuity. It is being able to stop digging in your heels against the tide of tomorrow. Theodore Roethke reminds us in *The Waking*, "We wake to sleep and take our waking slow, We learn by going where we have to go."

But here a "caveat." Trusting the process is a very different thing, a deeper thing, than "letting well enough alone." It is not the equivalent of Mr. McCawber's vacant optimism that "something will turn up." It is not a fatalistic "Que sera, sera." Trusting the process includes taking responsibility for choice and for action. It is an awareness of and a response to the nudgings and promptings of grace, moment by moment, day by day. Recalling the canoe analogy, there are times you must paddle like crazy or jab at the shore, and there are times when you have a clear shot and you just coast down the river. But most of the time, in canoeing, in relationship, in living, it is a matter of using the light touch, exercising sensitivity, finesse, timing. Most of the time it means responding to the signals that come from the other— whether the other is a river, a lover, or life itself—the signals of hope or the signals of heartache.

Yes, heartaches, too. And the heartaches come hard. Somewhere Nietzsche says, "We must love our wounds." I am not certain what that means, but I think at least in part it means that the wounds, the suffering, the heartache are all a part of me, to be accepted as testament that my humanity is bound up with the humanity of others.

The heartache signals we are not the only person attempting to navigate the currents of living. Others are having as hard a time as we in trying to trust the process. We are all in the process together and perhaps, with a little more practice, we can help each other navigate with a bit more assurance.

"...And I feel above me the day - blind stars waiting with their light. For a time I rest in the grace of the world, and am free."

— Wendell Berry
*The Peace of Wild Things*

# SAFETY AND VULNERABILITY:
## The Delicate Balance

It was the end of a summer holiday. The year was 1979. The last summer before our son Tyler was to enter the University of Pennsylvania. We were returning from a morning on the beach. As we came within sight of the house Tyler broke into a run. I watched him race ahead, moving further and further from us. An ache started moving in me. My neck muscles tightened. I knew that I was going to cry. And the tears came.

I remembered feelings from my childhood. I was the little boy left at summer camp, my family driving off, leaving me to deal with my homesickness. I was surprised that my childhood vulnerabiliity should confront me again in a situation of role reversal. I told myself that it was time for my son to leave home, but that was no help. The prospect of his claiming a life beyond the family that had nurtured him left an empty place in me, and my tears were an indication of my own vulnerability at the prospect of change and loss.

No one seeks to be vulnerable. But if you are human vulnerability will find you. This is certainly one of the meanings of that gorgeous and multi-faceted story of Jacob left alone at Jabbok and confronted by a mysterious demon with whom he must wrestle. Who does not know what it is to be mugged by some awful power in the night? Who does not know what it is to feel an inner pain break through the bonds of polite control and leave you with your doubts, uncertainties, fears? Who does not know vulnerability?

My experience of vulnerability at the symbolic running off of my son surprised, stunned me. Growing up a New England Yankee, I was taught to deny and repress dark, negative feelings. I learned to hold in my tears, muffle my passions, cover my anger. My tendency still is to deny rather than admit to being hurt; surface harmony at the cost of

175

emotional honesty. I struggle to admit to being vulnerable. I struggle *because* I have come to the realization that vulnerability (like that demon with which Jacob wrestled) can carry a blessing within itself. My vulnerability can be a source of generative energy, breaking through my angst and anger, pouring out in my tears.

On occasions when I summon the courage to identify with that which haunts me, to embrace the inner stranger, I am open to experience a transformation. I can be strengthened, enriched. When I can admit my fears to another person who is willing to honor them, to hold them up for me to look at, *then* those fears can even become friendly.

This is hardly an original notion. It is a staple of psycho-analysis, of pastoral counselling, even of children's litera-ture. Maurice Sendak's superb story, "Where the Wild Things Are," concerns a boy named Max who, having been sent to bed without his supper for behaving like a wild thing, travels to where the wild things are. He confronts these fearsome folk, staring right into their enormous yellow eyes. They become friendly, elect Max king, and proceed to have a jolly time together, all before Max returns home and finds his supper waiting.

Acceptance of vulnerability does more than awaken us to the ache within our hearts. It exposes us to the ache throb-bing in the heart of the world. Vulnerability keeps us engaged, invested, hurting, and, therefore, hoping. It keeps us from retreating into cold detachment and uncaring cyni-cism. Vulnerability keeps us from self-pity, sentimentality, and from taking either ourselves or our causes too seriously.

To be vulnerable is to suffer loss and to acknowledge and accept the grief in life as common to all. Buddhist teaching incorporates the parable of Kisa Gotami, a mother whose child had died and whose grief was inconsolable. She visited the Buddha, seeking counsel and relief from her feelings of utter hopelessness and despair. The Buddha assured her of his help, but first she must bring him a handful of mustard seed from the house of one who had not known the death of a loved one. Kisa Gotami went, carrying her dead son from house to house, seeking the magical mustard seed. But every home she visited contained a tale of anguish, of a close death. She returned to the Buddha empty-handed, having buried her child in a forest home, but not empty-hearted. She understood how her own grief and loss bonded her with the universal and with those she had visited, in the human network of shared, mutual vulnerability.

Kisa Gotami was freed of her sorrow by participating in sorrow. To be vulnerable is to have our own judgmental spirit broken repeatedly by the acknowledgment of our own failures and betrayals. To be vulnerable is to lose our immunity against the cries of others. When we become vulnerable we are accessible to being known. In the film "Tootsie" actor Dustin Hoffman accomplishes the transformation from being unemployed actor Mr. Michael Dorsay to being Ms. Dorothy Michaels, glamorous and sought-after TV sensation. Hoffman not only imitates a woman, he takes on a feminine persona and confesses his own surprise at what is happening to him. In an early scene he is combing the wig that he wears as "Dorothy" and comments to his roommate, "I think Dorothy is smarter than I am." After he has revealed his masquerade he attempts to re-establish a relationship with the woman to whom his "feminine" understanding and sympathy have made him "a friend." She says, "I miss Dorothy." He replies, "I miss her, too." But then he goes on to tell her that he can do all the things that "Dorothy" did, he just has to learn to do them "without the dress."

*To be human is to be vulnerable!*

But to be continually, totally vulnerable is to be dehumanized.

The wisdom of this correlative truth aids in understanding the more grotesque examples of inhumanity arising out of the fury of utterly vulnerable people. The scene is a black township bordering a South African city. An outraged crowd vents its rage upon a black township administrator who has been identified as a traitor to his people and a creation of the white power structure by whom he is

177

employed. He is sentenced by a kangaroo court to be executed by "necklace." An automobile tire soaked in gasoline is looped over the man's head and pinions his arms. The tire is ignited. The crowd cheers.

The spectacle is savage, bestial. Nothing can condone it. In addition to being a hideous fact of mid-1980s township life, the "necklace" is a symbol of the dehumanization of that life, lived by a people made utterly vulnerable by their powerlessness to deal with their oppression and forced to act out their frustration in subhuman initiatives. Testimony to the truth that constant, total vulnerability is dehumanizing.

The testimony is repeated worldwide. A Palestinian youth hurls a rock at an Israeli soldier, the soldier fires his automatic weapon, and the "Intifada" claim another martyr. Two British soldiers, blundering into an IRA funeral, are dragged from their car, beaten and executed.

Should the Palestinian throw the rock? Should the grieving Irish set upon the British soldiers? Such questions miss the point. Like the township blacks of South Africa, the Palestinians and the Irish see themselves as all but totally vulnerable to those who dominate their lives. To be totally vulnerable is to be dehumanized. Our humanity depends upon our having achieved some means of personal and social safety.

And I include the need for spiritual safety along with our need for social and personal safety.

I think of the old gospel hymn, "Leaning on the Everlasting Arms," which assured the singer of being held "safe and secure from all alarms". It does not appear in Unitarian Universalist hymnals. Religious liberals disparage such sentiment—at least in formal gatherings for worship. But there are other occasions—conferences, retreats—when those gathered around the piano in the evening will sing such a hymn with gusto and zeal.

I confess that until I came to know my own needs for safety, I associated such sentiments with weakness, a psychological crutch. I may differ about the manner of expression, *but* I now know that there is a time for sanctuary, for oasis, for shelter, for "the Everlasting Arms." I know there is a time for licking wounds, for restoring the soul, for waiting for strength to be renewed. I know there is a time for being safe.

If, in Jungian terms, the masculine God calls us out of our safety to leave home, the feminine God calls us out of our vulnerability to come home. And blessed are those who have ears to hear their calling. Safety and vulnerability are really inseparable. The rock of our safety lodges in the rapids of our vulnerability.

# TO HEAR THE MUSIC
## WHEN OUR OWN SONGS CEASE

*"Lead us, O God, to see a way where there is no path;*
*Give us to hear the music when our own songs cease.*
*And when the warm touch of life forsakes us*
*and our courage melts away,*
*May we stumble through the darkness unto Thee."*

I first recited this prayer (composed by A. Powell Davies of Washington, D.C.) in the context of memorial services. It speaks directly to people who grieve. However, its meaning extends to persons who experience all manner of psychological and spiritual exhaustion and diminishment. The prayer for us when the music has gone out of our lives and we feel out of touch with life itself.

*Summer Wishes, Winter Dreams,* is a film about two such people. Rita and Harry have been married for 24 years. Long enough for the habit of boredom to erode their relationship. Harry is an oculist, who at the beginning of the film is examining Rita's eyes. As he adjusts one of those machines which oculists use his hand accidentally brushes against Rita's cheek, and she recoils from this unexpected contact. It is a small, inconsequential incident, but enough to indicate that Rita and Harry have lost touch with each other. We soon learn that Rita and Harry have lost touch with just about everything. They both live in the past. In fact, they are *addicted* to the past. Somewhere in their 24 years of marriage the songs of these two people ceased—a fact which is neither very bad nor very unusual.

There are periods in every life, no matter how richly furnished with love and fulfilling relationships when, because of loss, pain, tragedy, the thousands of natural shocks that flesh is heir to, our songs cease and we cannot bring ourselves to "make our own kind of music." The problem with Rita and Harry is not that their songs have ceased, but that neither can hear the music of life that surrounds them because their lives contain no resonance for the present. *That* is their tragedy.

Erik Erikson laid groundwork for studies on how we develop, marking eight stages through which each of us must pass during our lives. Each stage is marked by a crisis. According to Erikson, each of us must engage, struggle, and eventually resolve that crisis in order to proceed to the next developmental stage. By the time we get to stage seven or eight, we know who we are and where we are and why we are. Or, as James Thurber told us, there are three things we ought to learn before we die: What we are running from, and to, and why.

Erikson describes the final, eighth stage in these words: "Only the person who has taken care of things and people and who has adapted to the triumphs and the disappointments which adhere to being, only in that person may the fruit of the previous seven stages gradually ripen." He continues, "I know of no better phrase to describe this ripening than 'ego integrity'." Someone asked Dr. Erikson to name the opposite of "ego integrity." He responded, "despair," the feeling that the time is now too short to start again, or to try and find an alternative route to "ego integrity." It is that kind of despair that gripped Rita and Harry. Trapped in an emotionally stifling past, they are unable to live in the present and unable to envision a future.

As a cleric I encounter echoes of this in people struggling out of leaden circumstances, trying to hear the music again. I meet them frequently in a most unlikely circumstance— the pre-marriage conversation with the minister. A circumstance which one would expect to be bright, sunny and cloud-free. Let it be noted that many of the people who come to Unitarian Universalist ministers to be married come as previously divorced persons. Asking a prospective bride or groom to speak about the previous marriage often opens a Pandora's box of pain and despair with which he or she is still struggling.

These conversations are difficult, but I am convinced that

it is irresponsible to ignore or avoid the painful past. When it is ignored, pain and despair have a way of re-asserting themselves in the context of the new relationship—often in more virulent and destructive froms. And so we talk about it. One man described his experience by saying, "I kept rediscovering the bottom. I'd think things can't get any worse, and then they'd get worse."

A divorce is only *one* of a myriad of ways our songs can cease and the music of life is silenced for us. One of the most important tasks for any church community is to provide means whereby people can again experience life's music when their songs have been interrupted. Being together in sharing, affirming, supportive and sustaining relationships can help even the most emotionally tone deaf among us to perceive the tune. And yet, there are rare times and situations when no degree of sharing can increase life's resonance. There are times when people *prevent* life's music from penetrating. There are situations, historical, personal, sociological, and political as well as psychological, in which whole peoples feel imprisoned in a leaden, unacoustic atmosphere. And yet, even in the worst of such circumstances, life's music has a way of creeping in.

When I served as minister to three small Unitarian communities in South Africa during the 1960s, each time a voice in our midst would sing of liberation and justice (e.g., author Olive Shreiner; Helen Joseph (the first white woman to be banned and placed under house arrest in South Africa) or Albert Luthuli (the first black Nobel Peace laureate) their songs only confirmed the lack of music in the larger society.

Suddenly, into that deadening silence burst a singer whose song awakened the music in so many of us. It was during the period of great U.S. civil rights angst that Attorney General Robert Kennedy was invited to lecture at the University of Cape Town. Kennedy spent only three days in South Africa. During that time he repeatedly called for a new human agenda and new approaches to old problems. He embodied a joy and an enthusiasm for life and for people which awakened resonances in even the most cynical. The story of those three days filled the South African press for weeks, but my favorite Robert Kennedy story was never published. It was told to me by a South African journalist who accompanied the Kennedy party around South Africa and focused on an incident in a hotel room in the city of Durban at 2 o'clock in the morning.

Kennedy had finished his fourth speaking engagement of that evening and returned to his hotel exhausted. He was scheduled to meet with Albert Luthuli and had to be awakened at 5 a.m. However, some of his staff had arranged for a troup of Zulu dancers and singers to entertain him. They had waited, so despite the hour Kennedy said he would see them, and he gave them enthusiastic attention. When they finished, his staff tried to hustle the group out, with perfunctory thanks. Kennedy interrupted, telling the staff, friends and assembled members of the press that those people had gone to great trouble to entertain and, therefore, he and his staff should repay them in kind. Whereupon Attorney General Robert Kennedy led his retinue in singing, "We Shall Overcome," to an astonished group of Zulus, South African Press persons, and Durban hotel staff, at 3 a.m. on a South African morning.

I suggest to you that one meaning of the word "prophet" should be in reference to a person who awakens the music in a situation so deadened that those trapped in the situation cannot acknowledge the possibility of music, let alone make it. A prophet is one who comes into a situation from the outside (from the psychic and spiritual "outside") whose song is so life affirming that it has the power to penetrate and break open sound-proofed lives and sound-proofed societies. A prophet is a person who can jump start the heart!

There remains an underlying meaning and lasting significance in the Jesse Jackson presidential campaign. The Rev. Jackson has been singing a song that is stirring and compelling not only for blacks but for the disadvantaged and the disenchanted, the rural poor and the marginally employed. Jackson has been singing to a society that has seen housing and domestic programs gutted, social and health programs reduced to minimal operations, inner cities near collapse, and a new, potentially permanent underclass of homeless and poverty-ridden people (many of whom are women and children) created in astonishing numbers. Jackson has been singing to a society which has seen the bottom line profits of large corporations shoot up while providing little for the middle class and crumbs to the working poor.

During the 1988 U.S. presidential primary campaign a letter appeared in the *New York Times* which spoke to this situation. One explanation of Mr. Jackson's success, wrote the author, is that those on the lower end of the spectrum have little confidence that any of the other Democratic candidates would, or even care to, act to turn the situation around. But those same people clearly believe that Jesse Jackson would. The letter writer continued: "I would not like to see Jesse Jackson nominated, but welcome his representation of an otherwise disenfranchised group in dealing with the Democratic elite. I'm concerned about some of his ideas of foreign policy and his coziness with leaders like Fidel Castro and groups like the PLO. His hip-shooting comments like referring to New York as 'Hymietown' are unfortunate, and some of his proposals appear to me too radical for mainstream America. I am not black, poor, disadvantaged or blue collar. I might not vote for Mr. Jackson, but I can understand why millions would, and I wonder if the leaders of the Democratic Party understand this."

During the period of primary campaigns my wife, Cathe, and I had dinner with *New York Times* columnist Anthony Lewis and his wife, Margi Marshall. Several weeks earlier Mr. Lewis had published an op-ed piece critical of the Jackson phenomenon and calling attention to Jackson's un-electibility. Before arriving at the Lewis' door, I pinned a campaign button ostentatiously proclaiming, "White Middle Class Males For Jesse." He laughed and asked if I'd seen his piece on Jackson. Not only had I seen it, I had admired it as I admire most of what he writes. Our differences are of a different magnitude. Anthony Lewis's profession demands that he be concerned with probability. My profession demands that I be concerned with possibility.

I believe that in the final analysis it does come down to a question of possibility; the possibility of hearing the music in the most extreme circumstances, "when the warm touch of life forsakes us and our courage melts." This possibility is really put to the test for us in that most personal of crucibles, the experience of the dying, the isolating experience of death for which we really have no language. And yet even in the context of terminal illness those who work intimately with the dying report a profound rhythm whereby the grappling turns intangibly into a dance, and resistance is transformed into acceptance.

I am invited to witness or to share in such moments. I listen to intimate testimony, to music in the abyss. In one such testimony: I found Stanley sitting with his soul and body scars, wondering if it were all not too much to pay. A feeding tube protruded from one side of his neck—on the other a tumor bloomed like a blood-soaked piece of cauliflower. Stanley was meticulous and organized—a career military man who had founded his own business after retirement. But who can organize a tumor that ravages your neck and throat—that will not let you swallow or eat and isolates you from your wife of many years? There he sat, staring at the wall. "It is so ugly," he said. "How can Shirley look at this one more day?" It was a question he could only tell to the wall until his fear of isolation overcame his fear of an answer. And Shirley's answer was simple. "It's ugly, but I see you when I dress the wound. I take care of you, not the tumor." Their hands trembled in one another's. Such direct conversation was not their style, but the moment demanded that the most important things be said now. And so they recited a kind of lover's litany. "I love you, thank you, I'm sorry, and good-bye." He never struggled with ugliness again.

*"Lead us O God to see the way where there is no path;*
*Give us to hear the music when our own songs cease.*
*And when the warm touch of life forsakes us and our*
*courage melts away,*
*May we stumble through the darkness unto Thee."*

Amen.

Mail Order Information:

For additional copies of STATIONS OF THE SPIRIT send $10.00 per book plus $1.50 for shipping and handling (in CA add 6½% sales tax). Make checks payable to Victor Carpenter, c/o First Unitarian Society, 1187 Franklin St., San Francisco, California 94104. Telephone (415) 776-4580.

Also available through local bookstores that use R.R. Bowker Company BOOKS IN PRINT catalogue system. Order through publisher SUNFLOWER INK for bookstore discount.